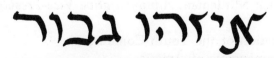

אֵיזֶהוּ גִבּוֹר

JEWISH LEADERSHIP AND HEROISM

Rabbi Jack Moline

Edited by Jonah Layman

UNITED SYNAGOGUE OF AMERICA
DEPARTMENT OF YOUTH ACTIVITES

UNITED SYNAGOGUE OF AMERICA
DEPARTMENT OF YOUTH ACTIVITIES

Rabbi Paul Freedman, *Director*
Jules A. Gutin, *Assistant Director*
Mirjam Mundstzuk-Ohrbach, *Projects Director*
Elliot Forchheimer, *Activities Director*
Martin S. Kunoff, *Activities Administrator*
Daniel B. Ripps, *Kadima Director*
Amy Katz Wasser, *Projects Coordinator*
Yitzchak Jacobsen, *Director, Israel Office*
Hezki Arieli, *Central Shaliah*
Jonah Layman, *Educational Consultant*

INTERNATIONAL YOUTH COMMISSION

Dr. Saul Shapiro, *Chairman*
Jeremy J. Fingerman, *Vice-Chairman*

UNITED SYNAGOGUE OF AMERICA

Franklin D. Kreutzer, *President*
Rabbi Jerome M. Epstein, *Senior Vice-President
and Chief Executive Officer*
Rabbi Benjamin Z. Kreitman,
Executive Vice-President
Jack Mittleman, *Administrative Vice-President*

A publication of the Youth Commission,
United Synagogue of America.
155 Fifth Avenue, New York, New York 10010.

Manufactured in the United States of America.
Typography and Lithography by Star Composition, Inc.
Cover design by Rhonda Jacobs Kahn.

Library of Congress Catalog Card Number: 87-051274

DEDICATION

to my teacher,
leader and heroine,

Ann Moline

"Her mouth speaks wisdom and the teaching of lovingkindness is on her tongue."

(Proverbs 31:26)

פיה פתחה בחכמה ותורת חסד על לשונה

and to our children,

Jennie and Julia

"Many daughters have met challenges, but you surpass them all"

(Proverbs 31:29)

רבות בנות עשו חיל ואת עלית על כלנה

ACKNOWLEDGMENTS

The editor wishes to thank the following publishers for granting reprint permission for material under their copyright:

For Chapter 6:

Excerpt from *Consolations For the Tribulations of Israel,* translated by Martin A. Cohen, © 1965, The Jewish Publication Society. pp. 37, 230.

Excerpt from *Sefer Ha-Qabbalah — The Book of Tradition* by Abraham Ibn Daud, translated by Gerson D. Cohen, © 1967, The Jewish Publication Society, p. 102.

Excerpts from *Masterpieces of Hebrew Literature,* edited by Curt Leviant, © 1969, KTAV. pp. 161, 164.

Excerpt from *The House of Nasi: Dona Grazia,* by Cecil Roth, © 1948, The Jewish Publication Society. p. 73.

For Chapter 7:

"The Golem", *A Treasury of Yiddish Stories,* edited by Irving Howe and Eliezer Greenberg. © 1953, 1954 by The Viking Press, Inc. All Rights Reserved. Reprinted by permission of Viking Penguin Inc.

For Chapter 8:

Excerpts from *Understanding Conservative Judaism,* by Robert Gordis, © 1978, the Rabbinical Assembly. Reprinted by permission of the Rabbinical Assembly. pp. 184, 194, 199.

RECOMMENDED READINGS

These books are good introductions to other Jewish heroes and leaders. Many more excellent sources are available on individuals in every period of Jewish history. The reader is encouraged to pursue in depth the life histories and accomplishments of leaders and heroes who are not included in this sourcebook.

Encyclopedia Judaica published by Keter Publishing House, Jerusalem, 1972.

International Hebrew Heritage Library, International Book Corp., Miami, 1969.

vol. 3: *Great Jews in Art*
vol. 4: *Jewish Nobel Prize Winners*
vol. 5: *Great Jews in Science*
vol. 6: *Great Jews in Performing Arts*
vol. 7: *Great Jewish Military Heroes*
vol. 8: *Great Jewish Statesmen*
vol. 9: *Great Sages of Judaism*
vol. 10: *Great Jews in Sports*

B'nai Brith Great Books Series, B'nai Brith Department of Adult Education, Washington, D.C., 1964.

vol. 1: *Great Jewish Personalities of Ancient and Medieval Times*
vol. 2: *Great Jewish Personalities of Modern Times*
vol. 3: *Great Jewish Thinkers of the Twentieth Century*

Davis, Moshe, The Emergence of Conservative Judaism, Jewish Publication Society, Philadelphia, 1963

Appendix A: "Biographical Sketches"

Koltun, Liz, *The Jewish Woman*, Schocken, New York, 1976.

"Models from Our Past"
"Women in Jewish Literature"

TABLE OF CONTENTS

EDITOR'S PREFACE

One way of learning about a society's values is by analyzing its leaders. A leader should embody all the values and ideals that his/her group holds dear to itself. If the group is a battalion of courageous, bold, and valient soldiers then one would not expect a coward to be its leader. The same could be applied to society as a whole.

This sourcebook will examine Jewish leaders and heroes throughout Jewish history. Over its 3500 year history Jewish civilization has had many leaders and heroes. What kind of people were they? Were they well respected by their Jewish constituents? What can we learn by examining the classic Jewish sources (e.g. Bible, Midrash, Talmud, etc.)? What kind of Jewish values can we learn from these Jewish leaders and heroes?

Rabbi Jack Moline has done an excellent job of examining the major figures of Jewish history and of challenging us with thought provoking questions. His thorough research is readily apparent by the wide range of sources incorporated in the text and his lucid writing style makes for an extremely readable volume. I thank him for his work. It was a pleasure to be involved in this book with him.

I would also like to thank the following people who have contributed valuable comments and suggestions.

Bobbie Berenbaum
Adena Cohen
Rabbi Jerome Epstein

Rabbi Paul Freedman
Marc Gary
Jules Gutin
Dr. Michael Korman
Rabbi Benjamin Kreitman
Rabbi Joel Roth

In addition I must express my gratitude to Dr. Stephen Garfinkel, Martin Kunoff, and Judith Sucher. They have helped in many ways in all aspects of the printing process. Finally, I am especially grateful to my wife Lenore for her support and understanding.

J.L.

FORWARD

I am especially grateful to the people who took the time to help me with this project. Any success is due, in great measure, to them. Any shortcomings are my own.

Jonah Layman was respectfully urgent in his supervision and review of my work. His enthusiasm and scholarship are a wonderful combination. Rabbi Stephen Garfinkel initiated my involvement in this project, adding my name to the roster of previous sourcebook authors. I am humbled in their company, and honored by Rabbi Garfinkel's confidence in me. The staff of the Department of Youth Activities of United Synagogue were of constant support, especially Rabbi Paul Freedman, Jules Gutin and Judith Sucher. Danny Siegel took an active interest in the source material, serving as a human compendium of *midrash* and *halakhah*. Dr. Miriam Shapiro helped me narrow the scope of the source book and offered the perspective of scholar and educator. All of the readers, who are acknowledged separately, aided me with their comments, but none so much as my rabbi, Prof. Joel Roth.

My good friend, Rabbi Lawrence Troster, is essentially responsible for Chapter 6, written out of the learning and expertise in medieval Jewish history he possesses.

My wife, Ann Moline, read and commented on every draft of every chapter. Her wisdom and insight, reflected in the final drafts, made me look good.

Finally, I express a special gratitude to the

students of my Confirmation Class at Agudas Achim Congregation in Alexandria, Virginia: Ellen Blank, Abby Friedman, Pam Hibler, Bobby Kaplan, Karyn Kasse, Leslie Lazarus, Abby Limmer, David Rosen, Brian Tureck and Tamara Wexler for their contributions as we studied this material together.

Rabbi Jack Moline
Cheshvan 5748

DEFINITIONS

We are going to begin by asking two questions:
   What is a hero?
   What is a leader?
You might think we are starting with the wrong questions. After all, heroes and leaders are people, and so the question might properly be phrased, as in *Pirkei Avot:*
   Who is a hero?
   Who is a leader?
It is important to define our terms first, because in doing so we make sure of two things. First, we agree on exactly what we are talking about, and second, we discover why this topic is so important.
   So what is a hero?
   We often associate the hero with courage or a noble purpose, especially performing acts which risk personal safety. A hero might also be a person prominent in some field or cause by virtue of special achievements or contributions.
   A hero stands out from the crowd because of something very special, yet very specific — an act of bravery, a discovery, an extra effort at a crucial moment.

And what is a leader?

A leader shows us the way by going in advance, guiding and directing by virtue of wisdom, experience or the confidence we place in him or her.

A leader stands at the head of the crowd because of qualities which are consistent and dependable, on which we come to rely. A leader seems to know where we are going, and how to get us there.

Heroes and leaders reflect the values of a society. We admire a hero because we would like to think that if we were in his or her position, we would have lived up to the hero's example. We would have thrown the touchdown pass, we would have rescued the drowning child, we would have told off the bigot, we would have stopped the enemy soldier. Each of those things in its own context is important because our society calls it important.

Yet, were we to visit a land with no football and try to explain the heroism of the quarterback, we would be met with blank stares. In a society in which bigotry is accepted, for example, where people are enslaved for being a particular race, speaking against such bigotry would be seen as foolish, not heroic. In a place which celebrated pacifism, the warrior might be greeted sadly rather than with admiration.

Leaders seem to have the skill to use the resoucres of a group, particularly the human resources, and direct them to a better realization of what the members of the group hold important. Whether the group is a sports team or a country, a club or a religious institution, we rely on the leader to show us how to best realize our goals, and sometimes even to set them for us.

Yet, some leaders use those special skills to misguide their followers, turning them into servants of their personal values. Other times, people who might be qualified to lead are denied the opportunity because of something beyond their control, quite often a strong value which conflicts with who they are.

A society which values men over women will have few female leaders. A society which values whites over blacks will have few black leaders. A society which values rich over poor, royalty over commoners, strong over weak will find its leaders among the favored groups. Very often, we can tell as much about a society's values from who is missing among the leadership as we can by who is included.

This is true in a positive sense as well. As we will see, Jewish society has valued wisdom over ignorance more often than not, and righteousness, courage, faithfulness and self-esteem over their opposites. As you proceed in your studies, please be aware that, try as we might, we cannot make history something it is not. The examples of leaders we have chosen reflect the values which have been present in Jewish society at various times, often including scholarship, piety and being a man. By examining our heroes and leaders we can learn more about who we were, who we are and who we will be.

A great deal has been written and discussed about the mechanics of leadership, but not quite so much about the values which should be present in leaders and heroes. Let us start with the title of this sourcebook as one example of an attempt to define the Jewish tradition's view of leadership.

Ben Zoma taught...	בֶּן זוֹמָא אוֹמֵר:
Who is a hero? One who	אֵיזֶהוּ גִבּוֹר? הַכּוֹבֵשׁ
	אֶת יִצְרוֹ שֶׁנֶּאֱמַר

15

conquers his passion[1], as it is written, "One who is slow to anger is better than a hero, and one who rules over his spirit than he who conquers a city." (Proverbs 16:32)

(משלי טז, לב): „טוֹב אֶרֶךְ אַפַּיִם מִגִּבּוֹר וּמֹשֵׁל בְּרוּחוֹ מִלֹּכֵד עִיר".

Ben Zoma's teaching represents the opinion of an individual teacher during a time of unusually severe persecution in second-century *Eretz Yisrael*. It is one of four such teachings, including "Who is wise? One who learns from every person... Who is wealthy? One who is satisfied with his lot... Who is honored? One who honors others..," which urge an individual to moderation. It is inspirational and reflects a way of thinking espoused by an earlier sage, Ben Sira, who suggested "seek not to understand that which is too difficult for you, for you have been shown more than you can understand."

In truth, however, the heroes and leaders represented in this sourcebook were not restrained, satisfied and excessively humble people. They were dreamers and schemers, often carried away by their passions and impulses. They broke new ground, or sought to regain old ground lost in times of trouble, they stood against the crowd, rather than blending into it.

Consider, for example, this passage from Tractate *B'rakhot* which recounts turbulent times in the study hall of the Talmudic sages at just the time Ben Zoma taught his maxim. Rabban Gamliel was the acknowledged leader and authority figure in the Jewish community. During his tenure, Roman

---

1) Some translate "inclination" or "evil impulse."

oppression was at its peak. Therefore, he used his authority freely to establish a unity among the Jews in practice and thought, apparently because he believed that dissent was dangerous in the face of outside persecution. Rabbi Joshua was a young and brilliant teacher who disagreed with some of Rabban Gamliel's teachings.

(Brakhot 27b-28a)

A student came to Rabbi Joshua and asked him if the evening prayer was optional or mandatory. He said it was optional. [The student] then went to Rabban Gamliel and asked him if the evening prayer was optional or mandatory. He said it was mandatory. [The student] said to him, "Didn't Rabbi Joshua tell me it was optional?" [Rabban Gamliel] said, "Wait until the warriors[2] enter the study hall."

When the warriors entered, the questioner stood and asked, "Is the evening prayer optional or mandatory?" Rabban Gamliel said to him, "It is mandatory." [Then] Rabban Gamliel said to them, "Is there anyone here who disputes this matter?" Rabbi Joshua replied, "No." [Rabban Gamliel] said

מעשה בתלמיד אחד
שבא לפני ר' יהושע
א"ל תפלת ערבית
רשות או חובה אמר
ליה רשות בא לפני
רבן גמליאל א"ל
תפלת ערבית רשות
או חובה א"ל חובה
א"ל והלא ר' יהושע
אמר לי רשות א"ל
המתן עד שיכנסו בעלי
תריסין לבית המדרש
כשנכנסו בעלי תריסין
עמד השואל ושאל
תפלת ערבית רשות
או חובה א"ל רבן
גמליאל חובה אמר
להם רבן גמליאל
לחכמים כלום יש אדם
שחולק בדבר זה אמר

---

2) "Warriors" refers to the scholars of the study hall.

to him, "Didn't they tell me you said it was optional?" He continued, "Joshua, stand up and let them testify against you!" Rabbi Joshua stood and said, "Were I alive and [the witness] dead, the living could contradict the dead. But since he is alive and I am alive, how can the living contradict the living (meaning, Yes, I said it)."

Rabban Gamliel continued to sit and teach and Rabbi Joshua remained standing until all of the people shouted to Chutzpit the Interpreter [who was announcing the teachings], "Stop!" And he stopped. They then said, "How long is [Rabban Gamliel] going to insult him?... Let us depose him!

"Whom shall we appoint instead? We cannot appoint Rabbi Joshua, because he is an involved party. We cannot appoint Rabbi Akiba lest Rabban Gamliel curse him because he has no family background. Let us therefore appoint Rabbi Elazar ben Azariah who is wise and rich and tenth in descent from Ezra... "

ליה ר' יהושע לאו
א"ל והלא משמך
אמרו לי רשות אמר
ליה יהושע עמוד על
רגליך ויעידו בך עמד
רבי יהושע על רגליו
ואמר אלמלא אני חי
והוא מת יכול החי
להכחיש את המת
ועכשיו שאני חי והוא
חי היאך יכול החי
להכחיש את החי היה
רבן גמליאל יושב
ודורש ור' יהושע
עומד על רגליו עד
שרננו כל העם ואמרו
לחוצפית התורגמן
עמוד ועמד אמרי עד
כמה נצעריה וניזיל ...
תא ונעבריה מאן
נוקים ליה נוקמיה
לרבי יהושע בעל
מעשה הוא נוקמיה
לר' עקיבא דילמא
עניש ליה דלית ליה
זכות אבות אלא
נוקמיה לר' אלעזר בן
עזריה דהוא חכם והוא
עשיר והוא עשירי
לעזרא ...

18

(Rabbi Elazar ben Azariah, who was a very young man at the time, reluctantly accepted the post of leader, but eventually shared it with Rabban Gamliel who apologized to Rabbi Joshua for his excesses.)

It is apparent from this story that the qualities articulated by Ben Zoma were hardly present in most of the principal characters. Rabban Gamliel hardly subdued his passion and even referred to the scholars as "warriors." Nor did he honor his colleague; he embarrassed him. When seeking a replacement for their leader because of his insensitivity, the values expressed by the scholars also do not reflect Ben Zoma's description: Rabbi Akiba has the wrong kind of family background and is therefore not "honored" enough; Rabbi Elazar ben Azariah is chosen for his book-learning, his material wealth and his "yichus" (family background), not his willingness to learn from all people nor his satisfaction with his lot nor his respect for others. Even Rabbi Joshua, the victim and, perhaps, hero of this story may have provoked the incident by challenging the teachings of his leader, Rabban Gamliel, as he had on two previous occasions. None of these men represent the humility and quiet dignity which Ben Zoma identifies with leadership!

Another illustration highlights the conflict between the real and the ideal. Moses Maimonides (Rambam) described the ideal king in his *Mishneh Torah*, the first code of Jewish law, which was compiled in 1180.

(Excerpts from Hilkhot M'lakhim uMilchamoteihem)

(1:1) Three *mitzvot* were commanded to Israel when

א. שלש מצוות נצטוו
ישראל בשעת כניסתן

19

they entered the land... (1:2) The selection of a king precedes the war [to obliterate] Amalek... and the destruction of the descendants of Amalek precedes the building of the Temple. Since the establishment of a king is a *mitzvah*, why is it that the Holy One did not want a king when the people asked it of Samuel? Because they asked for the king out of rebelliousness, not to fulfill the *mitzvah*, rather because they disliked Samuel the Prophet... (1:4) One must not appoint a king from among the converts... and not just the king, but all leaders of the Jews... . (1:8) ... This king must follow the ways of Torah and *mitzvah* and fight God's battles, for he is the king, and all of the *mitzvot* regarding kingship devolve upon him...

לארץ... ב. מינוי מלך קודם למלחמת עמלק... והכרתת זרע עמלק קודמת לבנין הבית. מאחר שהקמת מלך מצוה למה לא רצה הקב"ה כששאלו מלך משמואל. לפי ששאלו בתרעומת. ולא שאלו לקיים המצוה אלא מפני שקצו בשמואל הנביא. ד. אין מעמידין מלך מקהל גרים... ולא למלכות בלבד אלא לכל שררות שבישראל. ח. והיה אותו המלך הולך בדרך התורה והמצוה ונלחם מלחמות ה'. הרי זה מלך וכל מצות המלכות נוהגות בו.

Maimonides identified a system of priorities in the Torah which understood that the people needed effective and committed leadership before they could secure themselves in the land and before they could establish the presence of the Temple. The king must minimally meet four standards before he can be appointed:

    1. He must ascend to the throne to fulfill a *mitzvah*.

2. He must be born a Jew.
3. He must be pious.
4. He must be willing to fulfill the specific mitzvot of the king.

(Ibid.)

(2:1) The king is treated with great respect and puts fear and awe in the hearts of all people... (2:5) The king's hair is cut each day, he cares for himself and adorns himself with fine and fancy clothing... and he sits on his royal throne with a crown on his head, and the people should come to him whenever he desires and stand before him and bow to the ground... [except] for the high priest who [need] come only when he wants and... before whom the king stands... (2:6) [Yet with all this,]... Torah commands him to keep his heart within him humble and common... and not act too haughty among the Jews...

א. כבוד גדול נוהגין במלך. ומשמין לו אימה ויראה בלב כל אדם... ה. המלך מסתפר בכל יום. ומתקן עצמו ומתנאה במלבושין נאים ומפוארים... ויושב על כסא מלכותו בפלטרין שלו. ומשים כתר בראשו. וכל העם באין אליו בעת שירצה. ועומדין לפניו ומשתחוים ארצה... אבל כהן גדול אינו בא לפני המלך אלא אם רצה. ואינו עומד לפניו אלא המלך עומד לפני כהן גדול... ו. כדרך שחלק לו הכתוב הכבוד הגדול. וחייב הכל בכבודו. כך צוהו להיות לבו בקרבו שפל וחלל... ולא ינהג גסות לב בישראל יתר מדאי.

The king is to be shown the highest of respect, including all the trappings of his office. Though he is expected to maintain some humility, he is allowed to act "better" than anyone else except the High Priest — an interesting exception. However, along with the side benefits of his office, comes a greater responsibility.

(Ibid)

(3:1) During the time the king holds the throne, he must write for himself his own scroll of the Torah... which is only removed from his presence when he enters the bathroom, the bathhouse or any place inappropriate for reading from it... (3:2) He may not acquire an excessive number of wives. Common wisdom is that he may take up to eighteen wives, including concubines. And if he exceeds this number by even one, he is [punished by being] lashed... (3:3) He may not acquire an excessive number of horses... and if he does, he is lashed. (3:4) He may not acquire an excessive amount of silver and gold to place in his [official] coffers for his own sense of importance or pleasure, rather it shall be given to his soldiers, workers and servants...

א. בעת שישב המלך על כסא מלכותו. כותב לו ספר תורה לעצמו... (ו)לא יזוז מלפניו. אלא בעת שיכנס לבית הכסא. או לבית המרחץ. או למקום שאין ראוי לקריאה...

ב. לא ירבה לו נשים. מפי השמועה למדו שהוא לוקח עד שמונה עשרה נשים בין הנשים ופלגשים הכל שמונה עשרה. ואם הוסיף אחת ובעלה לוקה...

ג. ולא ירבה לו סוסים אלא כדי מרכבתו... ואם הוסיף לוקה.

ד. ולא ירבה לו כסף וזהב להניח בגנזיו ולהתגאות בו או להתנאות בו. אלא כדי שיתן לחיילותיו ולעבדיו ולשמשיו... ואם הרבה לוקה.

ה. המלך אסור לשתות דרך שכרות... אלא יהיה

and if he does, he is lashed. (3:5) The king is forbidden to get drunk... rather, he should be occupied with Torah and the needs of Israel day and night... (3:6) Similarly, he should not be [overly] occupied with women; even if he only has one wife, he should not be with her all of the time as the common folk[3] do...

עוסק בתורה ובצרכי ישראל ביום ובלילה... ו. וכן לא יהיה שטוף בנשים. אפילו לא היתה לו אלא אחת לא יהיה מצוי אצלה תמיד כשאר הטפשים...

The king has special moral responsibilities which, in spite of his political and military power, actually restrict him more than others. It was common in ancient times for a man to have many wives and/or concubines (women who bore him children). A wealthy man might have amassed quite a harem. The king was restricted to what today seems like an outrageous number — eighteen. When you consider that military and economic alliances were often made by official marriages between kings and princesses, this particular limitation has more ramifications than simply a curb on the king's desires.

Moreover, the king's personal behavior was strictly regulated. To be an appropriate leader, the conduct of his sex life, taxation and even his leisure hours were to be models of moderation and adherence to Torah. Excess was not allowed, and even the slightest infractions made him liable for a most

---

3) Even though this should be read "fools", the commentaries explain it as common folk.

humiliating form of public punishment!

Perhaps most startling of the powers Maimonides identifies with the kingship is his authority, in certain circumstances, to take the law into his own hands for the good of the people — as he perceives it. Though he makes it clear that this authority is limited to matters which do not contradict *mitzvot* found in the Torah, Maimonides claims:

(Ibid.)

(3:8) The king has permission to execute anyone who rebels against him, even if he merely decreed that a person should go to a certain place and he did not, or that a person must not leave his house and he left... (3:10) Anyone who kills another [and is not convicted under the very strict laws of the court], the king may execute him and thus improve the world according to the necessities of the times. He may execute many in a single day and hang them and leave them hanging for many days to instill fear and break the power of the wicked of the world.

ח. כל המורד במלך ישראל יש למלך רשות להרגו. אפילו גזר על אחד משאר העם שילך למקום פלוני ולא הלך או שלא יצא מביתו ויצא...

י. כל ההורג נפשות שלא בראיה ברורה. או בלא התראה. אפילו בעד אחד. או שונא שהרג בשגגה. יש למלך רשות להרגו ולתקן העולם כפי מה שהשעה צריכה. והורג רבים ביום אחד ותולה ומניחן תלויים ימים רבים להטיל אימה ולשבר יד רשעי העולם.

These extraordinary powers may help us understand why the king needed to be a person of exceptional self-control and deep reverence. If "power corrupts and absolute power corrupts absolutely," then the leader of the people of the covenant had to have certain checks and balances.

Once again, we find a conflict between the ideal as presented by Maimonides and the reality of history. Bear in mind that when Rambam wrote the *Mishneh Torah*, he was well aware of the excesses of the kings of Israel, from David's adultery to Solomon's hundreds of wives to the pagan practices and personal excesses of the later kings.

Maimonides tried to apply this standard of conduct to his own life. He was to a large extent successful. Though he never considered himself to be anything close to a king of the Jews, he nonetheless seems to have based his understanding of the ideal leader on what he himself felt capable of accomplishing as a human being. Moses Maimonides is an exceptional example of Jewish leadership, virtually without equal in Jewish history, much as Leonardo da Vinci set an unequaled standard for Renaissance Europe. Though he is not discussed at length in this sourcebook for the very reason that he represents a virtually unattainable ideal, he is worth your study and consideration for his unparalleled contributions to Jewish life.

At this point we have before us ideal qualities of leaders and heroes which are hard to achieve. After all, with very few exceptions, heroes emerge from particular situations. They are not selected on the basis of previous qualifications. You might contend that leaders are more likely to be chosen on the basis of their capabilities, but strength of character alone does not make for effective leadership. Indeed, the best leaders often emerge in the same way as heroes: out of a situation calling for their unique and sustained combination of talent, wisdom and power.

The research which went into this sourcebook turned up a surprising fact: comparatively little has been written which prescribes qualities for leaders. This is true for general society as well as Jewish society. Most of the sources available on the topic treat leadership functionally, that is, how someone can be most effective once he or she has reached a position of leadership, or they analyze the actions and motivations of past leaders and heroes.

It leaves us with a dilemma to consider before continuing: what shall we define as Jewish leadership and heroism? Shall we measure our examples against the ideals articulated by the likes of Ben Zoma and Maimonides, or shall we accept the examples of Jewish history as each contributing to a definition? Is anyone who performed a valiant service for the Jews a Jewish hero? (In fact, did he or she even have to be Jewish?) Shall we label any Jew who reached a position of leadership a Jewish leader, even if he or she did nothing particularly Jewish in that position, or served a community which was only partly Jewish?

The examples are many, from righteous gentiles during the Holocaust to assimilated Jews who served in diaspora governments, from Jews in professional sports to the sages of *Mishnaic* times who served the Roman government as judges. You should pause at this point to consider your own answer, given your own understanding of the issues.

As author of the sourcebook, I chose an approach which is as inclusive as possible. The historical leaders and heroes in chapters two through seven represent a cross-section of the ideal and the practical, the reluctant and the purposeful, the accidental and the predetermined leaders and heroes of our tradition. Most were Jewish, though not all.

Most were primarily involved in the particular life of the Jewish community, though not all. All of them had a mostly positive effect on Jewish life. By comparing the lives and actions of our people's leaders and heroes with the values we have expressed, I hope that we have the tools to evaluate those who are presented briefly in chapters eight and nine as today's leaders and heroes, and to come to some conclusions about our own roles, each of us, as leaders and heroes in our own rights.

Davids Thanksgiving

Chapter 2

TWO BIBLICAL LEADERS

DAVID, KING OF ISRAEL
AND DEBORAH THE JUDGE

The Bible is filled with examples of heroes and leaders. Finding two leaders who are representative is a difficult task, because quite often they are either so much larger than life that it is hard to imagine ourselves ever being like them, or there is an aspect of their lives which is emphasized by the biblical text which overwhelms our ability to see the person as a whole.

Abraham and Sarah, Isaac and Rebecca, Jacob and Rachel and Leah cannot really be considered leaders for the purposes of this book. Though they have influenced Jewish history throughout the generations, in their own time they really had no one to lead outside of their immediate families. Moses is such a towering figure in the Bible, primarily because of his personal conversations with God, that he is a difficult model to follow.

It is well accepted in our tradition that the best example of a leader in the Bible, outside of our earliest ancestors, is King David. His lifetime of accomplishments is documented in the Books of Samuel and the first Book of Kings, it is embellished in Chronicles,plus a great deal of *midrash* and legend. Most of the Book of Psalms is attributed to David by the tradition.Even if he himself did not write the psalms, they are called psalms of David because the tradition ascribes them to his musical and poetic styles. David also presided over a unified Jewish state, governed by the principles of Torah and benefiting from the voice of the prophets. It was an ideal and unique time in our history.

Deborah lived and taught in the time between the arrival in the Promised Land and the establishment of a kingdom. She was unique among the leaders of whom we have records in the Book of Judges: she was a woman. She, like David, combined talents of wisdom, strength and artistry. She brought to her position a sense of cunning and an understanding of the role of women in biblical society.

DAVID, KING OF ISRAEL
Life and Times

David lived almost 3000 years ago. He was born in Bethlehem to a man named Jesse of the tribe of Judah. Jesse was a man of some wealth, as he owned flocks and herds, and young David worked as a shepherd. During that time he developed his talent for music,his prowess in battle and his physical strength, for when he was summoned to the service of King Saul he both soothed him with his playing of the lyre and impressed him with his defeat of the enemy Philistine's champion Goliath. Saul welcomed David into his circle of close associates, and David became best of friends with Saul's son Jonathan, married Saul's daughter Michal, and added to his reputation as a valiant warrior through a number of successful campaigns against the Philistines. King Saul succumbed to the stresses of leadership and eventually went mad. He jealously imagined that David was trying to steal his throne and tried to have him killed a number of times. Each time David eluded him, we see that he added to his reputation as being protected by God.

Eventually, Saul and Jonathan were killed in battle. David had begun to set up his own power base in his native Judah, and after a series of intrigues involving Saul's successors, David assumed the kingship of a unified Israel. During the early part of his reign, he overcame the enemy who had plagued Saul: the Philistines. At the time, they were the only real power surrounding Israel, in part due to their use of iron weapons. Saul had tried to defeat them by attacking them head-on, and he was overpowered. David resorted to guerilla tactics, perhaps learned during his flights from King Saul. So complete was David's defeat of the Philistines that they are barely heard from again in history.

David organized the disunified tribes into a kingdom, moving the capital to Jerusalem. By creating a sense of the greater kingdom, David overcame, at least temporarily, the rivalries between the tribes They joined him in a series of foreign wars which crushed the weak surrounding nations and greatly expanded Israel's borders. To ensure loyalty, David replaced the volunteer army with paid professionals, including many foreign mercenaries, and paid them with tax money which he collected at increasingly higher rates from the people. Adding to the burden of the taxes was the bureaucracy set up by David to administer the kingdom — all sorts of ministers, scribes and secretaries — and the judges he appointed (of which he was the chief) to replace the fragmented tribal system of elders who sat in the gates of each city.

The quality and efficiency of life improved greatly in Israel during David's reign, but there was considerable discontent about the level of taxes and the changes in traditional practice among the people.

David was a man of great sensitivity to religion, but was not above using religion to further his plans for Israel, especially in three important ways. The first way was his return of the Ark of the Covenant to Jerusalem. The Ark had been captured by the Philistines, demoralizing the Israelites greatly. When David recaptured it and brought it to Jerusalem, there was great rejoicing and new spirit — and David succeeded in establishing Jerusalem as the capital of the kingdom. David wanted to build a Temple to God in Jerusalem, but listened to the advice of the prophet Nathan who opposed it.[1]

The second way was the taking of a census.[2] Relying on earlier tradition, yet violating an admonition in Torah, David accomplished what no other leader had since the settling of the Promised Land — a full count of the numbers in each of the tribes. Apparently, the tribes opposed the census for fear of losing land or influence. David succeeded, and then used the information to begin a program of forced service to the kingdom, a program which was increasingly resented, especially during the rule of later kings.

The third way was David's reestablishment of the Levitical cities of refuge. These cities, (which were

---

1. See IISam. ch. 6 and 7.
2. See IISam. ch. 24.

commanded to Moses), were to be under the supervision of the tribe of Levi, responsible for the ritual life of the people. There, a person who had accidentally killed another could remain safe from a relative of the victim seeking revenge. David accomplished two major political victories by restoring this important institution — he effectively ended the feuding between tribes and families which had created a climate of internal violence and distrust, and he scattered the Levites around the kingdom, reducing the power they had by virtue of their prestige and God-appointed roles.

Unfortunately, David's own household fell victim to the feuding he sought to end. Former members of Saul's loyalists continued their attacks on those who supported David. David's favorite son, Avshalom, brutally murdered his brother-in-law, Amnon, over a family grievance, and fled[3]. When Avshalom later returned to try to take over the kingdom, commander-in-chief Yoav (who was also David's nephew), killed him. David held the grudge against Yoav even to his death, and ordered Solomon to avenge his brother. David's reluctance to proclaim a successor led to a conflict between his sons Adoniyah and Solomon.

One more important event in David's life must be noted. He fell in love with a woman named Batsheva who was already married to a man named Uriah. Much as Saul had tried to do to him, David placed Uriah at the head of a forward dispatch of troops. Uriah died in battle and David married his widow. The prophet Nathan, respected enormously by David, condemned him to his face for what was

---

3. See IISam. ch. 13.

really a murder of convenience, and David was blemished by the event all the rest of his life.

David's Leadership Qualities

There are many lessons to be learned from David's life and times. In fact, there is a textbook on leadership to be written from the story of David's rise to power and his reign as king. From the synopsis of his life and your readings from the *Tenakh*, what qualities would you identify as David's strong points as a leader? Compare your answer to the question with the suggestions which follow.

1. David was apparently a creative genius. Not only was he talented musically and in writing poetry (psalms), he had the ability to approach problems and find innovative solutions to them. He defeated the Philistines by the use of guerilla strategy rather than raw strength. He diluted the power of rebel Levites by scattering them all over the kingdom. He developed a system of government services (a bureaucracy) to help justify a strong central government for the tribes.

2) David enjoyed the sympathies of the people. Even if his father had been wealthy, his reputation as a shepherd and a foot-soldier gained him support from among the common people, while his connections to the king by friendship and then marriage gave him acceptability to the local elite.

3) David was an attractive role model. There was much about him which others sought to imitate. He was a strong and valiant warrior and a leader of the troops. Moreover, though it is by no means necessary that a leader be physically attractive, the fact that the *Tenakh* recounts David's rugged good looks a number of times indicates that he was well known for being

physically appealing. His beauty added to his popularity.

4) David was willing to take risks. From his confrontation with Goliath to his encounters with Saul, from his wars of expansion to his institution of taxes, from his insistence on the census to his disposition of Uriah, David was willing to take chances to better his position of power and his personal life. Even if some of the risks seemed foolish or unethical, David was willing to assume the responsibility for them in order to meet a challenge.

5) David was a religious man. Every society has its own set of values which express what it considers to be most important in life (more on that later). For biblical Israel, those values were expressed in religious life. By practicing the rituals of Judaism and by honoring its symbols (the *Aron Kodesh*, prophets, religious poetry and, particularly, Torah), David established for the people that he believed strongly in the values they held dear.

6) David had a vision of unity for the people. His popularity, creativity and devotion to religion allowed David to pursue a policy of unifying the diverse and feuding tribes of Israel. Most of David's political acts seem bent on forging a coalition of the tribes and giving the people something in which they could all believe. For example, his wars of expansion gave the people an outside enemy on which to focus their aggressive energies, rather than each other. Similarly, he used the return of the *Aron Kodesh* to Jerusalem as a means of stirring the people's patriotism.

7) David was loyal. One reason David may have been so popular and effective a leader is that people knew they could count on him to be consistent. Even if he had plans to become king during Saul's reign, he never did anything to indicate that he was disloyal to

his father-in-law. Up to the last when he finally acknowledged his pledge to Batsheva that Solomon would be king, David's word was his bond.

It is important to take a moment here, as it will be each time we examine the qualities of a leader or a hero, to note that those things which make a leader *effective* do not necessarily make a leader *desirable*. You can probably think of many leaders in world history who have enjoyed David's wealth of leadership qualities and who have been cruel, evil or destructive. David himself had numerous character flaws — one of the most obvious being his lust for another man's wife — which made him far from perfect.

Perhaps you could add some other qualities which a leader should have to be effective. We would still be left with the problem of deciding what makes a leader or a hero desirable. Fortunately, that question has occupied our sages for a long time, as we have seen in a general context in the earlier excerpts from *Pirkei Avot* and Maimonides. Specifically, our sages have left us a wealth of *midrashim* about King David and many of our other early heroes and leaders which will serve as a basis of comparison for the other examples in this book.

Perhaps the earliest *midrashim* we have about King David are found in I Chronicles. There, David is depicted as a man of even greater religious sensibilities than in the books of Samuel and Kings. For example, the story of Solomon's ascent to the throne in David's declining days is told as a tale of intrigue and rivalry in the first section of I Kings. David is persuaded to fulfill his pledge to Batsheva and make Solomon king, and on his deathbed charges Solomon to be faithful to God's teachings, "walking in His ways and following His laws, His commandments, His rules and His

admonitions as recorded in the Teaching of Moses... "
(2:3). He also commands Solomon to avenge deaths
and insults for which David holds a grudge.

In Chronicles, however, David spends a great
deal of time as a vital leader preparing Solomon for
the tasks of succession, most importantly, the
building of the Temple, which God forbade David to
begin because he had "shed much blood and fought
many battles" (22:8). In Chronicles, David's last act
as king is to proclaim Solomon his successor and to
lead the people in worship, offering not just sacrifices,
but a magnificent spontaneous prayer. Nowhere is
there mention of the darker side of David's
instructions.

The Sages of the Talmud recognized David as
the best Jewish leadership could offer. He excelled in
every endeavor, not the least of which included a
familiarity with and dedication to Torah. Perhaps in
an attempt to understand what made him tick, or
perhaps to demonstrate what an ideal leader should
be, David became the subject of many midrashim
from Talmudic times.

Take as an example this interpretation of a verse
from Psalm 118, with which you are familiar because
of its inclusion in Hallel. The author of the midrash
seems to be asking the question "Why did David,
who wrote the Psalm, mention the gates of
righteousness, rather than the gate of righteousness?"

(Midrash Tehillim 118:17)

"Open the gates of righteousness to me" — In the World to Come they will say to each person, "How did you occupy	פתחו לי שערי צדק — לעולם הבא אמרו לו לאדם מה היה מלאכתך? והוא אומר מאכיל רעבים

37

yourself?" If he responds that he fed the hungry, they will say to him "This is the gate of God, the one who fed the hungry may enter." [If he said he] gave drink to the thirsty, they will say to him, "This is the gate of God, the one who gave drink to the thirsty may enter." [If he said he] clothed the naked... , raised orphans, gave charitably, performed acts of lovingkindness, [he will be rewarded] similarly. David said, "I did all of these things, let all [of the gates] be opened to me." Hence it says, "Open the gates of righteousness to me, I will enter them and praise God."

הייתי והם יאמרו לו זה
השער לה' מאכיל רעבים
הכנס בו משקה צמאים
הייתי והם אומרים לו זה
השער לה' משקה צמאים
הכנס בו מלביש ערומים
הייתי והם אומרים לו זה
השער לה' מלביש
ערומים הכנס בו וכן
מגדל יתומים וכן עושי
צדקה וכן גומלי חסדים
ודוד אמר אני עשיתי את
כולם יפתחו לי את כולם
לכך נאמר פתחו לי
שערי צדק אבוא בם
אודה יה.

David's remarkable career and unparalleled accomplishments could have led him to lay claim to righteousness by virtue of having slain the enemy Philistines, of returning the *Aron Kodesh* to Jerusalem, of having repented for his transgressions. Instead, the *midrash* contends, the qualities which made David our role model as a leader were his acts on behalf of the poor and downtrodden. He was judged not on his physical strength, but on his strength of character.

What prepared David for such a position? Another *midrash* suggests it was his early life as a herdsman.

David would bring the young goats to feed on the tops of the grasses which were tender; the older goats he would bring to feed on the mature grasses which were of medium consistency; he would bring the fully mature goats to feed on the roots of the grasses which were tough. The Holy One said, "One who knows so well how to herd the flock each according to its strength, he shall come to herd my flock — the people Israel."

הָיָה דָוִד כּוֹלֵא אֶת־הַצֹּאן אֵלּוּ מִפְּנֵי אֵלּוּ. הָיָה מוֹצִיא הַגְּדָיִים וּמַאֲכִילָם רָאשֵׁי עֲשָׂבִים, שֶׁהֵם רַכִּים, מוֹצִיא הַתְּיָשִׁים וּמַאֲכִילָם אֶמְצָעָם שֶׁל עֲשָׂבִים, שֶׁהוּא בֵּינוֹנִי, מוֹצִיא הַבַּחוּרִים וּמַאֲכִילָם עִקָּרָם שֶׁל עֲשָׂבִים, שֶׁהוּא קָשֶׁה. אָמַר הַקָּדוֹשׁ־בָּרוּךְ־ הוּא: מִי שֶׁהוּא יוֹדֵעַ לִרְעוֹת הַצֹּאן אִישׁ לְפִי כֹחוֹ — יָבֹא וְיִרְעֶה צֹאנִי, אֵלּוּ יִשְׂרָאֵל.

David is depicted as concerned for each member of the flock, be it the animals in his charge as herdsman or the people in his charge as king. In spite of evidence of his selfishness in the actual text of the *Tenakh*, the Sages attributed a selfless concern for others to him in their retelling of the story. Moreover, he was depicted as beloved of God beyond all others and devoted to Torah.

As an illustration, there is the *midrash* which recounts a conversation between David and God. David tries to persuade God to reveal the day of his death. God tells David only that he will die on *Shabbat* in his seventieth year. He pleads to live to Sunday, but God refuses to reduce Solomon's reign by even a day. He pleads to die on Friday so as to spend *Shabbat* in heaven. God responds:

"One day of your study of Torah is more pleasing to me than a thousand sacrifices which Solomon might offer to me on the altar."

[From then on, David] spent every *Shabbat* in the study of Torah. On the day that his time came to die, the Angel of Death stood before him, but could not take him because he wouldn't stop reciting his teachings. [The Angel] said, "What shall I do to him?" There was a garden behind the palace, and the Angel of death went and climbed into the trees and made a noise. David went out to see, and as he climbed a step, it crumbled beneath him, [distracting him from Torah], and his soul departed and he died.

טוֹב לִי יוֹם אֶחָד שֶׁאַתָּה יוֹשֵׁב וְעוֹסֵק בַּתּוֹרָה מֵאֶלֶף עוֹלוֹת שֶׁעָתִיד שְׁלֹמֹה בִּנְךָ לְהַקְרִיב לְפָנַי עַל גַּבֵּי הַמִּזְבֵּחַ.

כָּל יוֹמָא דְשַׁבְּתָא הֲוָה יָתִיב וְגָרֵיס כּוּלֵי יוֹמָא, הַהוּא יוֹמָא דְּבָעֵי לְמֵינַח נַפְשֵׁיהּ קָם מַלְאַךְ הַמָּוֶת קַמֵּיהּ וְלָא יָכֵיל לֵיהּ, דְּלָא הֲוָה פָּסַק פּוּמֵּיהּ מִגִּירְסָא. אֲמַר: מַאי אֲעַבֵּיד לֵיהּ? הֲוָה לֵיהּ בּוּסְתָּנָא אֲחוֹרֵי בֵּיתֵיהּ, אֲתָא מַלְאַךְ הַמָּוֶת סָלֵיק וּבָחֵישׁ בְּאִילָנֵי, נְפַק לְמֶיחֱזֵי. הֲוָה סָלֵיק בְּדַרְגָּא, אִיפְּחִית דַּרְגָּא מִתּוּתֵיהּ, אִישְׁתֵּיק וְנָח נַפְשֵׁיהּ.

It would appear that David was the consummate man to the Sages — not just successful in battle and leadership on a political level, but the ideal person as well. They seemed* to emphasize that his leadership was so effective not just because he had talent, but because he had good character as well — he was compassionate, scholarly and measured his own worth by the good he could do for others.

In fact, David seems almost too perfect. He was called *Mashiach*, the Anointed One, and the next Anointed One (or Messiah) was to come from the house of David. There was a very real danger that this human being could be seen as a god himself, and so there are *midrashim* which retreat from this too-good-to-be-true image of the king.

(*Yoma* 22b)

| Rav Yehudah said in the name of Shmu'el: Why didn't the house of Saul retain the kingship? Because there were no blemishes in it. | אמר רב יהודה אמר שמואל מפני מה לא נמשכה מלכות בית שאול מפני שלא היה בו שום דופי. |

What were David's "blemishes"? Remember that when Saul lost the kingship, David was still a young man who had not yet committed the sins he would later regret. As great as David was, there was an element of arrogance to him which prevented him from reaching "perfection". He questions God's wisdom in creating spiders, then wasps , then in allowing insanity into the world. In each case God proves the value of these creations by having them save David's life in a moment of crisis. Perhaps the ultimate arrogance, however, was David's complaint to God about his reputation:

(*Sanhedrin* 107a)

| [David] once complained to God: "O Master of the | אָמַר לְפָנָיו: רִבּוֹנוֹ שֶׁל עוֹלָם, מִפְּנֵי מָה |

Universe, why do people say 'God of Abraham, God of Isaac, God of Jacob,' but not 'God of David?' " The answer came, "[Abraham, Isaac and Jacob] were tested by me [to prove their faith], but yours has not been proved." David pleaded, "Then examine me and try me, O God." ... And God said, "I will test you and I shall even grant to you what I did not grant [the Forefathers]. I shall tell you beforehand that you shall fall into temptation at the hands of a woman."

אוֹמְרִים, ,,אֱלֹהֵי אַבְרָהָם אֱלֹהֵי יִצְחָק וֵאלֹהֵי יַעֲקֹב" וְאֵין אוֹמְרִים אֱלֹהֵי דָוִד? — אָמַר: אִינְהוּ מִינַּסוּ לִי, וְאַתְּ לָא מִינַּסִית לִי, אָמַר לְפָנָיו: רִבּוֹנוֹ שֶׁל עוֹלָם, בְּחָנֵנִי וְנַסֵּנִי... אָמַר: מִינַּסְנָא לָךְ, וְעָבִידְנָא מִילְתָא בַּהֲדָךְ, דִּלְדִידְהוּ לָא הוֹדַעְתִּינְהוּ וְאִילוּ אֲנָא קָא מוֹדַעֲנָא לָךְ, דִּמְנַסֵּינָא לָךְ בִּדְבַר עֶרְוָה.

Other "blemishes" are ascribed to David as well. He was, according to the Sages, without many true friends once Jonathan died. During the rebellion of his son, Avshalom, the *midrash* contends that a handful of non-Jews were among the only ones who proved their loyalty to David. His transgression involving Batsheva left him spiritually and physically isolated (he became a leper) for many years. But perhaps most alarming is the reason given in the *midrash* as to why David was not permitted to build the Temple:

(*Ruth Zuta* 51)

David's wrong in connection to the famine (which plagued

השליכו עליו בנות ישראל את כל הכסף

the people during his reign) lay in his not having applied his private wealth to reducing the people's suffering... He put [it] aside for use in building the Temple, and even during three years' famine this fund was not touched. God said, "You refrained from rescuing human beings from death in order to save your money for the Temple. So, the Temple will not be built by you, but by Solomon."

והזהב, והקדישו לבית המקדש, וכיון שבא רעב שלש שנים, בקשו ממנו ישראל ליתן ולא רצה ליתן להם כלום. אמר לו הקב״ה לא קבלת עליך להחיות בו עניים, חייך אין אתה בונה אותו, אלא על ידי שלמה בנך.

DEBORAH THE JUDGE

The story of Deborah is found in the book of Judges, chapters 4 and 5. Unlike the story of David, which is greatly detailed, we know relatively little about Deborah.

Deborah lived during the period of the Judges, which followed the conquest of Canaan by Joshua and the generation of Israelites who entered the Promised Land. It was a period of ups and downs for the tribes. The beginning of the book recounts how generations of Israelites were disloyal to God, and how leaders emerged to return them to obedient ways and to repel the military enemies. Deborah was just such a leader.

(Judges 4:4-9)

Deborah, the wife of Lappidot, was a

וּדְבוֹרָה אִשָּׁה נְבִיאָה אֵשֶׁת לַפִּידוֹת הִיא שֹׁפְטָה אֶת־

prophetess; she led Israel at that time. She used to sit under the Palm of Deborah, between Ramah and Bethel in the hill country of Ephraim, and the Israelites would come to her for decisions. She summoned Barak, the son of Avinoam, of Kedesh in Naphtali and said to him, "The Lord, the God of Israel has commanded: Go march up to Mount Tabor and take with you ten thousand men of Naphtali and Zevulun. And I will draw Sisera, Yavin's army commander, with his chariots and troops, toward you up to the Wadi Kishon; and I will deliver him into your hands." But Barak said to her, "If you go with me, I will go; if not, I will not go." "Very well, I will go with you," she answered. "However, there will be no glory for you in the course you are taking, for then the Lord will deliver Sisera into the hands of a woman." So Deborah went with Barak to Kedesh.

יִשְׂרָאֵל בָּעֵת הַהִיא: וְהִיא
יוֹשֶׁבֶת תַּחַת־תֹּמֶר דְּבוֹרָה
בֵּין הָרָמָה וּבֵין בֵּית־אֵל
בְּהַר אֶפְרָיִם וַיַּעֲלוּ אֵלֶיהָ
בְּנֵי יִשְׂרָאֵל לַמִּשְׁפָּט:
וַתִּשְׁלַח וַתִּקְרָא לְבָרָק בֶּן־
אֲבִינֹעַם מִקֶּדֶשׁ נַפְתָּלִי
וַתֹּאמֶר אֵלָיו הֲלֹא־צִוָּה
יהוה אֱלֹהֵי־יִשְׂרָאֵל לֵךְ
וּמָשַׁכְתָּ בְּהַר תָּבוֹר וְלָקַחְתָּ
עִמְּךָ עֲשֶׂרֶת אֲלָפִים אִישׁ
מִבְּנֵי נַפְתָּלִי וּמִבְּנֵי זְבֻלוּן:
וּמָשַׁכְתִּי אֵלֶיךָ אֶל־נַחַל
קִישׁוֹן אֶת־סִיסְרָא שַׂר־צְבָא
יָבִין וְאֶת־רִכְבּוֹ וְאֶת־הֲמוֹנוֹ
וּנְתַתִּיהוּ בְּיָדֶךָ: וַיֹּאמֶר
אֵלֶיהָ בָּרָק אִם־תֵּלְכִי עִמִּי
וְהָלָכְתִּי וְאִם־לֹא תֵלְכִי עִמִּי
לֹא אֵלֵךְ: וַתֹּאמֶר הָלֹךְ
אֵלֵךְ עִמָּךְ אֶפֶס כִּי לֹא
תִהְיֶה תִּפְאַרְתְּךָ עַל־הַדֶּרֶךְ
אֲשֶׁר אַתָּה הוֹלֵךְ כִּי בְיַד־
אִשָּׁה יִמְכֹּר יהוה אֶת־
סִיסְרָא וַתָּקָם דְּבוֹרָה וַתֵּלֶךְ
עִם־בָּרָק קֶדְשָׁה:

There are a number of qualities which seem to

make Deborah a leader. Compare your list with the one that follows.

1) Deborah had the gift of prophecy. It is difficult for us in our day and age to understand the power of prophecy. We may consider the prophet to have received direct communication from God or we may consider the prophet to have been a person of unique wisdom and insight. In either case, in her own time, Deborah's Divine gifts commanded respect from her fellow Israelites.

2) Deborah was wise. It was not easy for a woman to become educated at Deborah's time — she must have spent many hours eavesdropping on conversations among the men and the retelling of the stories of the history of the Israelites and their understanding of God's law. The application of knowledge is wisdom, and Deborah was respected for her ability to apply her knowledge to real situations.

3) Deborah established a recognizable leadership style. She sat beneath a palm tree known by her name and dispensed advice to those who approached her. She may have been among the first people to have an "office." By consistent practice, she made herself accessible and available to the people.

4) Deborah was bold. As a woman, she was at a natural disadvantage in biblical society. Yet, she did not hesitate to "summon" Barak and, in God's name, command him to raise an army. Deborah's aggressiveness made her effective.

5) Deborah was a shrewd judge of human nature. She carefully baited Barak when he hesitated to follow her advice, cunningly warning him that his victory would be attributed to a woman, and not to his military skill. By doing so, she put him in a situation in which he needed to succeed — to prove her wrong, if nothing else.

The Sages attributed to Deborah other qualities which this brief description of her life and times could not really justify. Still, their assumptions about what such a woman at such a time would have had to have been can give us an insight into how they viewed the ideal leader.

(*Megilla* 14a and Rashi)

"And she sat beneath a palm tree... " Why does it state "a palm tree"? Rabbi Shimon ben Avshalom taught: Because of [the suspicion of] intercourse.

Rashi comments: It is tall and casts no shade, so a man could not [be suspected of attempting to] have intercourse with her as he might in a house.

והיא יושבת תחת תומר מאי שנא תחת תומר אמר ר' שמעון בן אבשלום משום יחוד

משום יחוד. שהוא גבוה ואין לו צל ואין אדם יכול להתייחד שם עמה כמו בבית.

Deborah took great pains to eliminate even the appearance of improper personal behavior, according to the *midrash*. Even though she was a married woman and a respected judge, the public perception of men coming and going from her house would have compromised her credibility in a society which valued the integrity of marriage and proper personal conduct.

Deborah's gift of prophecy came as a result of her piety, one *midrash* suggests. Playing on the phrase *eishet lappidot*, which means "the wife of Lappidot", the Sages suggested that *lappidot* should be understood in its literal sense, meaning "torches". Deborah was known, therefore, as "a woman of torches", making the wicks for the lights which burned in the Tabernacle. God rewarded her for making the wicks extra-thick to shed light longer on the sacrifices by giving her the gift of enlightenment (that is, prophecy). For going beyond the letter of the law in her "woman's work", Deborah becomes a leader among her people.

Still, there was a sense of something being wrong with Deborah's generation to begin with that they did not merit a man for a leader. "Woe to the generation which has a woman as its leader," says *Midrash Tehillim*, echoing Deborah's self-mocking challenge to Barak.

DAVID AND DEBORAH AS PERSONAL ROLE MODLES

What can the stories of David and Deborah — especially with the embellishments of the Sages — do for us in our understanding of the world in which we live? At this point, it would be worthwhile to return to the lists of attributes and deficits of each of these two leaders and ask some relevant questions:

1) We no longer have kings, and judges are very different in our society than they were thousands of years ago. Are these qualities particular to biblical times and circumstances, or can they apply to leaders in our own day and age?

2) Are David's and Deborah's positive qualities attributes which only leaders should have? Need a person be a head of state or societal leader — or want to be — to cultivate those qualities? Is there a value in trying to develop the positive traits in our own lives?

3) How do the descriptions, both biblical and *midrashic*, of David and Deborah fit the definitions in the first section? How do they relate to the advice of Ben Zoma and Maimonides?

*Symbols of the Twelve Tribes

48

TWO BIBLICAL HEROES

In this chapter, two very different types of people will be introduced as examples of heroes, people who responded admirably in unique circumstances. Judah, the son of Jacob, played a major role in the story of Joseph's sale to the Ishmaelites. Rachav, a non-Israelite resident of Jericho, was a key figure in the conquest of Canaan by Joshua's army.

Keep in mind these questions as you study the two heroes:

1) Did he/she act in the best interests of the community? Who benefited from the heroic actions? Did anyone suffer for his/her heroism? If so, was the action worth the suffering?

2) Would you have recommended the same course of action if Judah or Rachav had sought your advice?

3) Were there Jewish values expressed through this heroism? Were there Jewish values violated?

JUDAH, SON OF JACOB

Jacob was the third of our patriarchs. He was the

father of thirteen children, twelve of them sons, by four different women who were his wives or concubines. His favorite wife was Rachel, and her elder son was Joseph. Jacob favored Joseph above all his other children, including those who were older than he. Resentment grew among the brothers, and eventually they plotted to kill their spoiled and arrogant brother one day when he came out to the fields in which they worked:

(Genesis 37:19-27)

And they said to one another, "Look, this dreamer is coming. Now let us kill him and throw him into one of the pits, and we will say, 'An evil beast has devoured him.' We will see what becomes of his dreams." And Reuven heard it and rescued him from them and said, "Let us not take his life." And Reuven said to them, "Shed no blood. Throw him into this pit in the wilderness, but do not lay a hand on him." [He meant] to rescue him from their hands and return him to his father. So when Joseph came to his brothers, they stripped Joseph of his coat of many colors which he was wearing, and they took him and threw him into the pit, an

וַיֹּאמְרוּ אִישׁ אֶל־אָחִיו הִנֵּה בַּעַל הַחֲלֹמוֹת הַלָּזֶה בָּא: וְעַתָּה לְכוּ וְנַהַרְגֵהוּ וְנַשְׁלִכֵהוּ בְּאַחַד הַבֹּרוֹת וְאָמַרְנוּ חַיָּה רָעָה אֲכָלָתְהוּ וְנִרְאֶה מַה־יִּהְיוּ חֲלֹמֹתָיו: וַיִּשְׁמַע רְאוּבֵן וַיַּצִּלֵהוּ מִיָּדָם וַיֹּאמֶר לֹא נַכֶּנּוּ נָפֶשׁ: וַיֹּאמֶר אֲלֵהֶם רְאוּבֵן אַל־תִּשְׁפְּכוּ־דָם הַשְׁלִיכוּ אֹתוֹ אֶל־הַבּוֹר הַזֶּה אֲשֶׁר בַּמִּדְבָּר וְיָד אַל־תִּשְׁלְחוּ־בוֹ לְמַעַן הַצִּיל אֹתוֹ מִיָּדָם לַהֲשִׁיבוֹ אֶל־אָבִיו: וַיְהִי כַּאֲשֶׁר־בָּא יוֹסֵף אֶל־אֶחָיו וַיַּפְשִׁיטוּ אֶת־יוֹסֵף אֶת־כֻּתָּנְתּוֹ אֶת־כְּתֹנֶת הַפַּסִּים אֲשֶׁר עָלָיו: וַיִּקָּחֻהוּ וַיַּשְׁלִכוּ אֹתוֹ הַבֹּרָה וְהַבּוֹר רֵק אֵין בּוֹ

empty pit with no water. They sat down to eat bread and looked up and saw a band of Ishmaelites coming from Gil'ad, with their camels bearing spices, balm and jewels on their way down to Egypt. And Judah said to his brothers, "What is the profit in killing our brother and hiding his blood? Come, let us sell him to the Ishmaelites and let our hand not be upon him, for he is our brother, our flesh." And his brothers listened to him.

מָיִם: וַיֵּשְׁבוּ לֶאֱכָל־לֶחֶם
וַיִּשְׂאוּ עֵינֵיהֶם וַיִּרְאוּ וְהִנֵּה
אֹרְחַת יִשְׁמְעֵאלִים בָּאָה
מִגִּלְעָד וּגְמַלֵּיהֶם נֹשְׂאִים
נְכֹאת וּצְרִי וָלֹט הוֹלְכִים
לְהוֹרִיד מִצְרָיְמָה: וַיֹּאמֶר
יְהוּדָה אֶל־אֶחָיו מַה־בֶּצַע
כִּי נַהֲרֹג אֶת־אָחִינוּ וְכִסִּינוּ
אֶת־דָּמוֹ: לְכוּ וְנִמְכְּרֶנּוּ
לַיִּשְׁמְעֵאלִים וְיָדֵנוּ אַל־
תְּהִי־בוֹ כִּי־אָחִינוּ בְשָׂרֵנוּ
הוּא וַיִּשְׁמְעוּ אֶחָיו:

You might think, in reading this story the first time, that Reuven would have been the best choice for a hero. After all, Reuven not only prevented a murder, he had every intention of returning his brother to their father in one piece. What makes Judah the hero in this situation? He may have prevented Joseph's death (since he did not know of Reuven's secret plan), but he certainly sent his brother to an unknown future as a slave. Consider the questions above in light of this story.

The Sages were troubled by the same dilemma, and sought to explain Judah's actions in most positive terms. In one *midrash*, they explained that Judah's protest was part of the evidence that the Israelites observed the Ten Commandments even before the Torah was given, because Judah knew that we were not to commit murder! Building on this idea, Nachmanides offers his commentary that Reuven persuaded the brothers not to commit murder, but Judah convinced them that they would be just as guilty of murder by neglect as they would be by action.

Yet, the Sages still understood that Judah's actions did not go far enough. They draw this conclusion from the fact that the text says "And his brothers listened to him" — they would have listened had he said to rescue Joseph as well. He had started the process of redemption, but not completed it.

Judah's turn at heroism came again when the brothers were reunited in Egypt. Joseph had risen to the second highest office in the land, unbeknownst to his brothers who had come asking for food during a famine. To test their humanity, Joseph framed his youngest brother Benjamin for theft, and Judah, who had pledged his own life to Jacob as a guarantee of Benjamin's safety, was forced into action. The Torah recounts Judah's plea to Joseph, whose identity is still unknown to the brothers:

(*Genesis* 44:30-34)

Now when I come to your servant my father and the lad is not with us, seeing as his soul is bound up with the lad's soul, when he sees that the lad is not with us he will die. And your servants will bring down your gray-haired servant, our father, with sorrow to the grave. For your servant [Judah] became a guarantor for the lad to my father, saying, "If I do not	וְעַתָּה כְּבֹאִי אֶל־עַבְדְּךָ אָבִי וְהַנַּעַר אֵינֶנּוּ אִתָּנוּ וְנַפְשׁוֹ קְשׁוּרָה בְנַפְשׁוֹ: וְהָיָה כִּרְאוֹתוֹ כִּי־אֵין הַנַּעַר וָמֵת וְהוֹרִידוּ עֲבָדֶיךָ אֶת־שֵׂיבַת עַבְדְּךָ אָבִינוּ בְּיָגוֹן שְׁאֹלָה: כִּי עַבְדְּךָ עָרַב אֶת־הַנַּעַר מֵעִם אָבִי לֵאמֹר אִם־ לֹא אֲבִיאֶנּוּ אֵלֶיךָ

bring him to you, I will bear the blame to my father forever." Therefore, let your servant [Judah] be your slave instead of the lad, and let the lad go up with his brothers. For how shall I go up to my father if the lad is not with me, lest I see the evil which will befall my father?

וְחָטָאתִי לְאָבִי כָּל־הַיָּמִים: וְעַתָּה יֵשֶׁב־נָא עַבְדְּךָ תַּחַת הַנַּעַר עֶבֶד לַאדֹנִי וְהַנַּעַר יַעַל עִם־אֶחָיו: כִּי־אֵיךְ אֶעֱלֶה אֶל־אָבִי וְהַנַּעַר אֵינֶנּוּ אִתִּי פֶּן אֶרְאֶה בָרָע אֲשֶׁר יִמְצָא אֶת־אָבִי.

By volunteering to take the place of Benjamin whose fate would have mirrored Josephs's, Judah indicated his willingness to complete the process of redemption he had begun so long ago with Joseph.

What was the nature of Judah's heroism? There are three possibilities:

1) Judah was willing to sacrifice himself for the sake of someone he loved. In that sense, he was saving a life — not Benjamin's, because he would have lived as a slave, but Jacob's, because the loss of his youngest son would have broken his heart beyond repair.

2) Judah was willing to stand up for what was right in spite of his brothers' reluctance. In that sense, he went against the pressure of his peers, his brothers. In fact, one midrash says that Joseph wanted to know why Judah pleaded so much more than his older brothers. Judah responded that he had more at stake — perhaps not just his pledge to his father, but his sense of integrity.

3) Judah recognized the importance of sh'lom bayit, of peaceful family relationships. In demonstrating his concern for his father, he also melted Joseph's hardened heart and brought the brothers back together again.

With all this, it is important to remember that Judah himself never consistently acted as a leader. Though he had a certain influence with his brothers, he rarely exerted it in a positive way except in times of crisis. Another example worth studying on your own is his relationship with his daughter-in-law, Tamar, in which he is called to task for not using his proper authority (see Genesis chapter 38). Moreover, one *midrash* claims that Jacob suspected Judah of Joseph's murder — a clue to the nature of Judah's personality as the Sages perceived it.

RACHAV OF JERICHO

At the time the Israelites prepared to enter the Promised Land, Joshua, their commander, sent two spies to investigate the entry point at Jericho. They entered Jericho and took refuge in the house of a prostitute named Rachav, a native of the city. When the king's soldiers came to take the spies into custody, Rachav, apparently on her own initiative, hid them and told the soldiers that the spies had left the city, sending them on a wild goose chase toward the Jordan river.

(Joshua 2:9, 11b-13)

She said to the men, "I know that God has given you the land, and that fear of you has fallen upon us, and that the inhabitants of the land melt before you... for the Lord your God is God in

וַתֹּאמֶר אֶל־הָאֲנָשִׁים יָדַעְתִּי
כִּי־נָתַן יהוה לָכֶם אֶת־הָאָרֶץ
וְכִי־נָפְלָה אֵימַתְכֶם עָלֵינוּ וְכִי
נָמֹגוּ כָּל־יֹשְׁבֵי הָאָרֶץ
מִפְּנֵיכֶם:
כִּי יהוה אֱלֹהֵיכֶם הוּא
אֱלֹהִים בַּשָּׁמַיִם מִמַּעַל וְעַל־

the Heavens above and on the earth below. Now please swear to me by the Lord that since I dealt kindly with you, you will also deal kindly with my father's household — and give me a true symbol — by keeping alive my father, my mother, my brothers and my sisters, and all that is theirs, and save our lives."

הָאָרֶץ מִתָּחַת: וְעַתָּה
הִשָּׁבְעוּ־נָא לִי בַּיהוה כִּי־
עָשִׂיתִי עִמָּכֶם חָסֶד וַעֲשִׂיתֶם
גַּם־אַתֶּם עִם־בֵּית אָבִי חֶסֶד
וּנְתַתֶּם לִי אוֹת אֱמֶת:
וְהַחֲיִתֶם אֶת־אָבִי וְאֶת־אִמִּי
וְאֶת־אַחַי וְאֶת־אַחְיוֹתַי וְאֵת
כָּל־אֲשֶׁר לָהֶם וְהִצַּלְתֶּם אֶת־
נַפְשֹׁתֵינוּ מִמָּוֶת:

The spies indeed made a pact with Rachav. She was to tie a red thread to her window facing over the wall to the city, and those inside her house would be spared. When the city was overtaken and destroyed by the Israelites, Rachav and her household were escorted by the two spies to the Israelite camp where they were safe.

With the story of Rachav we face an interesting problem. Remember that one of the questions to ask about each hero is the effect the heroics had on the community. In this situation, Rachav did not act on behalf of her community, that is, Jericho. She acted on behalf of the advancing Israelites. What was to the benefit of the Israelites was to the decided disadvantage of her king and his subjects.

Moreover, it might appear that her motives were not pure. She secretly struck a deal with the spies to save her if they were successful in capturing the city. Obviously, if they were unsuccessful, her family would have survived as well! Look carefully again at her words to the spies. Is she merely impressed by the power of the Israelites and their God, or is she basically looking out for herself?

Bear in mind that it is emphasized a number of times that Rachav was a prostitute. Though prostitution seems to have been a more acceptable activity in pagan society than it ever was in Jewish tradition, the constant repetition of Rachav's profession seems to cast a certain light on her actions, as if to say she would sell her loyalty the same as her sexual favors.

The Sages were apparently disturbed by this possibility. Some, including the later commentators, suggest that the Hebrew word *zonah*, meaning prostitute, really comes from the same root as *mazon*, meaning food. Therefore, they claim, Rachav was not a prostitute, but a person who provided food, that is, an inn-keeper.

Others suggest that the opportunity to serve God's cause turned Rachav away from her immoral life of many years, and she became a devoted follower of the God of Israel, so much so that Joshua married her!

Whatever the context of Rachav's life, there remains the basic question: what makes her a Jewish heroine?

JUDAH AND RACHAV AS PERSONAL ROLE MODELS

Both Judah and Rachav lived in times which were very different than our own. Yet, they acted heroically on behalf of the Jewish people under very difficult circumstances. These questions may be addressed as a method of determining some of the ways the actions of these two Biblical figures may apply to our own lives.

1) To whom do we owe allegiance when there is a

conflict of opportunities? Judah had to choose between his angry and violent brothers and his spoiled and arrogant brother. Rachav had to choose between the country of which she was a citizen and the nation of Israel. Their apparently "right" choices were in the interests of individual Jews and the Jews as a whole. But how might their choices be viewed by the beneficiaries of the "wrong" choices?

2) Is an act heroic only when performed by an unlikely hero, or is it heroic in and of itself? Neither Judah nor Rachav have very attractive character traits, and they lived among people who were much like themselves. Had nine of the ten brothers rejected a single brother's plan to kill Joseph, would Judah's participation have been heroic? If Rachav had been an "agent" of Joshua, planted in Jericho months before, would her actions have been heroic or merely a turn of duty?

3) Must a hero act out of a sense of "rightness," or can we separate the benefits of the actions from the motives of the person? If Judah sought to make a profit from the sale of Joseph, rather than to save his life, is he less a hero? If Rachav merely tried to save her skin, rather than to aid God's cause, is she less a heroine?

*An illustration of five men seated around a table eating. It is likely that it illustrates the text which recounts the five rabbis of B'nai Brak (including Rabbi Akiva).

Chapter 4

TWO RABBINIC LEADERS

RABBAN YOCHANAN BEN ZAKKAI AND RABBI AKIVA

The period of time during which the *Mishnah* and Talmud developed is called the Rabbinic Period. It began more than 2000 years ago and lasted until the sixth century of the common era. During this time, wrenching changes took place in the life of the Jews, especially during the first and second centuries CE, the years preceding and following the destruction of the Second Temple in Jerusalem.

The Roman Empire had expanded throughout the known world, and the Jewish nation was part of that Empire. Though the Romans had respect for the cultures and religions in their empire, they nonetheless sought to unify the various nations under their own idea of peace and culture. Nowhere were they less successful than in Rabbinic Palestine. At first, the Romans allowed great freedom of practice to the Jews, but as the Roman government became more insistent on conformity, many Jews resisted. Eventually, the Romans turned to violence to impose their will, instituting the death penalty for the teaching of Torah in certain places (notably Jerusalem) and defiling and then destroying the Holy Temple.

It was a critical time for the Jews. To that point, much of Judaism had been connected to the Temple, including the requirements of sacrifices and tithing (taxes for the Temple). The priests held a great deal of power and prestige and Jerusalem was the undeniable center of Torah and worship. With Jerusalem embattled and then destroyed, Judaism might have disintegrated (as the Romans hoped). Obviously, it did not.

Judaism survived in great part because of some extraordinary leaders and heroes of the time. Faced with increasingly difficult circumstances, they helped make a transition from Temple-centered ritual to day-to-day personal practice, from an idea of God as "dwelling" in the Temple to one of God being present in every place.

Both Rabban Yochanan ben Zakkai and Rabbi Akiva lived during this crucial juncture in Jewish history. Both of them knew the relative peace and prosperity before the Temple was destroyed (though Akiva was a very young man), both of them lived through the destruction of the Temple, both of them took steps to continue the dynamic of Jewish survival outside of Jerusalem. Perhaps of special importance to you, the reader, is this common trait of Yochanan and Akiva: both of them became leaders by virtue of their own efforts, not by who they knew nor by government appointment.

RABBAN YOCHANAN BEN ZAKKAI

We do not know much of anything about the background of Rabban Yochanan. His father's name is all the formation we have of his family, and we know not ng about his place of birth. He is said to have been a student of Hillel.(In fact, it is suggested in the Tal nud that he was the least of Hillel's eighty students in spite of the fact that he was well-versed and brilliant in every aspect of the tradition.)

One *midrash* says that he lived 120 years, spending forty years each in business, study and teaching. While it is questionable that he actually divided his life so neatly, it is likely that he spent a substantial portion of his life in business before he undertook the intense study of Torah required for the title Rabban (Rabbi). After studying in Jerusalem, he went to live in the Galilee in a small town called Arav, where he was not called upon to use his scholarship very much. Unhappy with the Galilee, he returned to Jerusalem.

At the time, the *Sanhedrin* was organized in a way designed to create cooperation between the two different classes in Palestinian society. The Pharisees (Rabbis) came from both classes: the wealthy land-owners and the poorer shepherds who owned no land. To emphasize the belief that both classes were equal, there were two leaders of the *Sanhedrin* — the *Nasi* (President) and the *Av Bet Din* (Head of the Court), who assisted the *Nasi*. If one was a land-owner, the other was a shepherd. Rabban Yochanan ben Zakkai represented the common class as *Av Bet Din* under Rabban Shim'on ben Gamliel. He used his influence to reduce the special privileges which came with wealth, especially among the priests who were not sympathetic as a group to the Pharisees. His wisdom and logic persuaded many of them to accept the authority of the Rabbis, and he became a person of exceptional influence even outside of his own students, affecting even the Temple ritual.

It was during his administration that the Romans laid siege to Jerusalem to bring it under their rule. Though he had spent his years as teacher avoiding both conflict and contact with the Romans and urging peace among the various authorities, it became evident to him that Jerusalem was doomed. He knew that if the Temple and the *Sanhedrin* were destroyed, there would be no center to hold Jews and Judaism together.

Rabban Yochanan therefore pretended to be sick, and pretended to die. Dressed in burial shrouds and carried out of the city for burial past the Roman soldiers, he went to ask a favor of the Roman governor, Vespasian, who was intrigued by his escape from Jerusalem. He asked for permission to preserve the school at Yavneh, a town already under Roman control. Vespasian was apparently amused by the modest request and granted it.

Rabban Yochanan went to work establishing Yavneh as the new center of Jewish authority, developing an approach to teaching and practicing Judaism that was not dependent on the Temple. There was considerable opposition to his actions at first, especially since he declared the rulings of the court in Yavneh to be as authoritative as those which used to come from Jerusalem. Eventually, the opposition fell away, and Rabban Gamliel, who had become the last *Nasi* in Jerusalem, came to Yavneh to assume that position.

Rabban Yochanan never became the head of the academy at Yavneh, but his influence was felt both in his teachings and in the institution which was built due to his foresight. He survived only ten years or so after the destruction of the Temple.

RABBAN YOCHANAN BEN ZAKKAI'S CAREER AS A LEADER

One of Rabban Yochanan's students was Rabbi Chanina ben Dosa who had a reputation as being very pious and holy. This *midrash* gives us an insight into the attitude Rabban Yochanan had toward the importance of Torah.

(Brakhot 34b)

The son of Rabban Yochanan ben Zakkai took sick. [Rabban Yochanan] said to [Rabbi Chanina], "Chanina, my son, pray for mercy for him so that he may live." He put his head between his knees and prayed for mercy for him and he lived. Rabban Yochanan ben Zakkai said, "If ben Zakkai had put his head between his knees all day long, [God] wouldn't have noticed him." His wife said to him, "Is Chanina greater than you?" He replied, "No; but he is like a servant before the king and I am like a prince before the king."

חלה בנו של רבן יוחנן
בן זכאי אמר לו חנינא
בני בקש עליו רחמים
ויחיה הניח ראשו בין
ברכיו ובקש עליו
רחמים וחיה אמר רבן
יוחנן בן זכאי אלמלא
הטיח בן זכאי את
ראשו בין ברכיו כל
היום כלו לא היו
משגיחים עליו אמרה
לו אשתו וכי חנינא
גדול ממך אמר לה
לאו אלא הוא דומה
כעבד לפני המלך ואני
דומה כשר לפני
המלך.

The king's servant may appear before the king at any time. Rabban Yochanan saw Rabbi Chanina's piety as "serving" God. But the prince may only appear before the king when he is summoned or at appointed times. It is to such a prince that Rabban Yochanan compares himself.

Which is preferable? Each serves his purpose — certainly Rabbi Chaninah was a hero to Rabban Yochanan and his family — but the leaders of the people, the princes who represent the interests of the king, are those who are versed in Torah. Rabban Yochanan seemed to believe that knowledge was a more important leadership quality than spirituality. To put it another way, wisdom qualifies a person to be a leader more than influence.

Rabban Yochanan seemed to be aware of the ability of a leader to shape public attitudes and opinions. Perhaps he understood the power which that gave him, and he appeared to use it carefully. For example, when he taught, he consistently used verses from the *Tenakh* to support his rulings, even if they might be accepted on the basis of his reputation as a scholar alone. He gave as his reason that later generations might disregard a ruling which had no Biblical grounding.

Yet, in spite of his caution in teaching, he spoke out forthrightly on matters which affected public practice, using the full force of his learning and powers of persuasion. Here is an example of a dispute he had with the Temple priests, members of a sect called the Sadducees, over whether scrolls of the *Tenakh* made one's hands ritually unclean when handled. The dispute may seem trivial to you at first glance, but try to read it for the larger point Rabban Yochanan tries to make.

The Sadducees said, "We have a complaint about you Pharisees! You say that the holy books make the hands unclean, but ordinary books[1] do not make the hands[ritually] unclean." Rabban Yochanan ben Zakkai said, "This is all? Don't you say that the bones of a donkey (an unclean animal) are clean, but bones of the High Priest Yochanan are unclean?" They said to him, "Because they are precious they are unclean, so that a person not use the bones of his father or mother to make eating utensils." He said to them, "So, too, the holy books, which, because they are precious, are unclean. But ordinary books, which are not precious — they do not make the hands unclean."

אוֹמְרִים צָדוּקִים: קוֹבְלִין אָנוּ עֲלֵיכֶם פְּרוּשִׁים! שֶׁאַתֶּם אוֹמְרִים: כִּתְבֵי הַקֹּדֶשׁ מְטַמְּאִין אֶת הַיָּדַיִם, וְסִפְרֵי־הָמֵירָס אֵינָם מְטַמְּאִים אֶת הַיָּדַיִם. אָמַר רַבָּן יוֹחָנָן בֶּן זַכַּאי: וְכִי אֵין לָנוּ עַל הַפְּרוּשִׁים אֶלָּא זוֹ בִּלְבָד? הֲרֵי הֵם אוֹמְרִים: עַצְמוֹת חֲמוֹר טְהוֹרִים, וְעַצְמוֹת יוֹחָנָן כֹּהֵן גָּדוֹל טְמֵאִים. אָמְרוּ לוֹ: לְפִי חִבָּתָן הִיא טֻמְאָתָן, שֶׁלֹּא יַעֲשֶׂה אָדָם עַצְמוֹת אָבִיו וְאִמּוֹ תַּרְוָדוֹת. אָמַר לָהֶם: אַף כִּתְבֵי הַקֹּדֶשׁ לְפִי חִבָּתָן הִיא טֻמְאָתָן, וְסִפְרֵי הָמֵירָס שֶׁאֵינָן חֲבִיבִין — אֵינָן מְטַמְּאִין אֶת הַיָּדַיִם.

Rabban Yochanan's ruling had far-reaching effects. First of all, it helped to bring some of the priests into sympathy with the Pharisees, increasing the influence of the Sages. Second, it established that

1) literally, "the writings of Homeras".

one may not eat while studying the holy texts, because it was forbidden to eat with hands which were ritually unclean (this is why we wash and say a *brakha* before eating). This ruling ensured that proper care and respect would be given to the books. But more importantly, it established in the minds of the community the importance of Torah. This principle became all the more important after the Temple was destroyed.

In the first section of the book, one of the definitions offered of a leader suggested that he or she seemed to know in which direction we were going. This quality was part of Rabban Yochanan's make-up as well. Here, as an example, is the reasoning he offered for the discontinuation of the ritual of *sotah*, which was used to determine if a wife had been unfaithful to her husband.

(Tosefta Sotah 14:2)

With the increase of the number of adulterers, an end was put to the ceremony of *sotah*, for the ceremony of *sotah* applies only in doubtful cases, whereas now there has increased the number of those who are openly guilty of [adultery].	משרבו המנאפין פסקו מי מרים לפי שאין מי מרים באין אלא על הספק עכשיו כבר רבו הרואין בגלוי

The *Mishnah (Sotah 9:9)* suggests that Rabban Yochanan himself discontinued the ritual for the reason above. Whether he was responsible for the discontinuation or merely expressed the reason for it, he made a shocking statement about the nature of Jewish life and the direction it was taking. *Sotah* is a ritual commanded in the Torah. The lifestyles of the Jews of his times had, in effect, negated the power of Torah! We have no way of knowing whether the incidence of adultery lowered following his statement, but he obviously had become a respected source of moral guidance.

What kind of person was Rabban Yochanan ben Zakkai? It is said that he constantly occupied himself with Torah, in all his conversations and thoughts, and never hurried his studies unless *Pesach* or *Yom Kippur* was that evening. He was a voracious student and learned in every aspect of the tradition — written, oral, mystical and practical. With all his scholarship, however, including the non-Jews of his acquaintance, he was personally modest, never allowing another person to open the door for his students in his place, and insisting, even at the peak of his influence in Yavneh, that it was much more important to show honor to the assembly than to himself.

The influence of these personal characteristics is apparent in this saying of the scholars of Yavneh:

(Brakhot 17a)

I am God's creation and my fellow [the simple peasant] is God's creation. My work is in the city and his work is in the field. I awaken early for my work and he awakens for his work. Just as he does not intrude on my work, so do I not intrude on his work. If you were to say I do much	אני בריה וחברי בריה אני מלאכתי בעיר והוא מלאכתו בשדה אני משכים למלאכתי והוא משכים למלאכתו כשם שהוא אינו מתגדר במלאכתי כך אני איני מתגדר

and he does little [to increase Torah], remember the teaching, "Much or little, it is all the same, so long as one's intentions are Godly."

במלאכתו ושמא תאמר אני מרבה והוא ממעיט שנינו אחד המרבה ואחד הממעיט ובלבד שיכוין לבו לשמים.

Rabbi Yochanan ben Zakkai was also not afraid to take bold steps in the name of preserving the tradition. A whole series of *mishnayot* in the fourth chapter of tractate *Rosh haShanah* describe the innovations introduced by Rabban Yochanan in the course of his early years of influence in Yavneh. Deprived of the Temple, he decreed that some rituals previously reserved for the Temple itself be allowed in Yavneh, and liberalized certain other rituals which were dependent on the unique circumstances of Jerusalem.

For example, he decreed that the *shofar* could be sounded when *Shabbat* coincided with *Rosh haShanah* not just in Jerusalem but in Yavneh. By extension, his students understood him to mean in any place where the *Bet Din* was headquartered. He decreed that the *lulav* and *etrog* were to be used each day of *Sukkot* in all localities as a remembrance of the Temple. Previously, they had been used only on the first day outside of the Temple. He also set aside the second day of *Pesach* for a special observance in remembrance of the Temple. On that day, the first wave-offering of the new harvest, an *omer* of grain, was brought for use in the Temple. After the ceremony of thanksgiving, it was permitted to eat from the harvest. Rabban Yochanan prohibited the new harvest on the day of its first offering as a regular reminder of the missing Temple.

Once again it is essential to view these innovations in the light of their times. Ritual practice was the only area over which Jewish authorities still had full power under Roman rule. That power had been limited to the priests and the *Sanhedrin* in Jerusalem, which were effectively destroyed by the Romans. Rabban Yochanan ben Zakkai's decrees established the idea that just as God is not limited to any one place or time, so is the study and practice of God's law not limited to any one place or time. *Shofar*, *lulav* and *omer* were immensely popular rituals. By selecting such powerful symbols on which to take his stands, Rabban Yochanan ben Zakkai was able to increase the effectiveness of his message to all the people and gain popular support for them. The message was expressed even more powerfully in this exchange between Rabban Yochanan and his student, Rabbi Yeshoshua, who despaired when he saw the ruins of the Temple.

(Avod d'Rabbi Natan ch. 4)

"Woe to us," cried Rabbi Yehoshua, "for this, the place where the sins of Israel could be atoned for, is destroyed!" [Rabban Yochanan] said to him, "My son, do not grieve. We have another way to atone as effective as this. And what is it? It is acts of loving-kindness, as it is said, For I desire mercy and not sacrifice' (Hosea 6:6)."

אמר ר' יהושע אוי לנו
על זה שהוא חרב
מקום שמכפרים בו
עונותיהם של ישראל.
א"ל בני אל ירע לך
שיש לנו כפרה אחת
שהיא כמותה ואיזה
זה גמ"ח שנאמר כי
חסד חפצתי ולא זבח

Rabban Yochanan ben Zakkai's personality seems to be virtually perfect: scholarly, compassionate, principled, charismatic and bold enough to take chances. You may find yourself suspicious that such a person could ever really have lived. He did indeed live, but it is unlikely that anyone could be so close to perfection throughout his life. What is more likely is that those aspects of his life and career which made him so effective and positive a leader were emphasized by his students throughout the ages in order to teach us about the qualities they saw as desirable in a leader. Take some time now to identify those qualities, and see how they compare with the previous lists of David's and Deborah's leadership qualities. Ask yourself about the similarities and differences: what they are and why they are.

1) Rabban Yochanan ben Zakkai was a well-rounded person. He nurtured his interests in all aspects of Jewish learning, and had experience in the world of business as well. His expertise was not limited to a few aspects of his society.

2) He was deferential to others. Whether he was dealing with the Roman authorities before the destruction of Jerusalem or with people in the street or with his own students, Rabban Yochanan showed them respect. Even in situations in which he had obviously higher status, he nonetheless honored every person.

3) He was both learned and wise. Some people gather much knowledge but cannot apply it; some people seem to have a knack for practical problems but lack the background to understand them fully. Rabban Yochanan ben Zakkai blended both positive traits.

4) He was an activist. Though Rabban Yochanan had a history of deferring to others, when his insight

led him to believe action was necessary, he took it. He was willing to be the guide to others during both crisis and calm by showing the way.

5) He was a model of personal morality. Rabban Yochanan ben Zakkai conducted his personal life in a way that prompted the respect and admiration of others. This included his modesty and reliance on Torah for guidance rather than the arrogance of egotism.

6) Rabban Yochanan ben Zakkai understood and was willing to use the powerful symbols of his culture to further society. As we read, he shamelessly exploited for holy purposes the power of Temple rituals both before and after its destruction. The best example is the symbolic message of how he escaped Jerusalem to establish Yavneh: he "rose from the dead," just as Judaism did after the siege of Jerusalem.

RABBI AKIVA

Just after the death of Rabban Yochanan ben Zakkai there appeared at Yavneh a man named Akiva. He was more than forty years old at the time and had never studied in much depth. Before too long, he had become one of the most important leaders in Jewish history.

Akiva ben Yosef was born in Judea, probably around the year 50. At the time, there was no system of schools for children, and Yosef was probably unable to teach his son anything but the simple sheep herding skills by which he earned his living. Akiva could not read a single letter. When he became a young man he took a job herding the sheep of a wealthy neighbor, Kalba Sabua. There he attracted the eye of the boss's daughter, Rachel.

They wanted to be married, but she refused unless he agreed to give up his life of ignorance and study with the scholars. In spite of the objections of her father, who disowned them, they were married and Akiva began to study. He was close to forty years old.

As you can imagine, it was extremely difficult for Akiva to start from *alef-bet* as an adult. In fact, it was only after his son reached an educable age that Akiva began to learn — he hired a teacher to instruct them both together. Once he overcame his initial ignorance, studies came much more easily to him and he mastered the legal sections of Torah and then the rest of *Tenakh*. He was prepared to begin studies at the rabbinical academy at Yavneh.

At first, he had trouble finding a mentor (someone who would take a special interest in him). Rabbi Eliezer ben Hyrkanos would not take on poor students. Rabbi Yehoshua ben Chanania did not challenge him enough. Rabbi Tarfon, who later became Akiva's close friend, came from a wealthy family, and the two men did not see eye to eye on important issues of the day. Finally he began to study with Nachum of Gamzo who taught him a new method of interpreting Torah which ascribed significance to every single letter, a method Akiva would use his entire life. He then returned to Yavneh where Rabbi Eliezer finally accepted him as a student.

From this point on, Rabbi Akiva grew in esteem and influence in Jewish society. He is credited with the first full systematization of the *halakhah* and *aggadah*. He traveled to Rome to plead the cause of Jewish vitality. He became a central figure in passive resistance to Roman oppression.

One *midrash* suggests that Rabbi Akiva lived for 120 years, divided into three periods of forty years each: as shepherd, student and leader. (This is an interesting comparison to Rabban Yochanan ben Zakkai.) What is true is that Rabbi Akiva's return to Yavneh signaled the beginning of a remarkable career as a leader, both in scholarship and politics. He played a key role in revitalizing Judaism as it reeled under the tragedies and indignities of Roman oppression, giving Jewish law a new and dynamic role in everyday life and using it as a vehicle for political resistance. Rabbi Akiva died the death of a martyr — tortured by the Romans for violating their ban on teaching Torah.

RABBI AKIVA'S CAREER AS A LEADER

In a sense, it is remarkable that Akiva agreed to study at all. In his later years he admitted to some deep-seated prejudices against scholars. Perhaps he felt that they wasted their time; perhaps he blamed their obstinacy for the tribulations visited by the Romans; perhaps he was merely jealous of their learning. In any event, he once told his students:

(Pesachim 49b)

"When I was ignorant I said that if someone would give me a scholar I would bite him like an ass." His students said, "Rabbi, you should have said 'like a dog.'" He said to them, "This one (the ass) bites and breaks the bone, but that one bites but does not break the bone."	תניא אמר רבי עקיבא כשהייתי עם הארץ אמרתי מי יתן לי תלמיד חכם ואנשכנו כחמור אמרו לו תלמידיו רבי אמור ככלב אמר להן זה נושך ושובר עצם וזה נושך ואינו שובר עצם:

73

Rabbi Akiva seemed to have a knack for approaching old problems in new and aggressive ways. The *Mishnah* (*Pesachim* 6:2) recounts what may have been the first of Rabbi Akiva's rulings to have been accepted at Yavneh. Rabbi Eliezer suggested that if a certain activity (in this case the *Pesach* sacrifice) prohibited on Shabbat but necessary to the Temple service was permitted within the Temple on *Shabbat*, then other activities connected to it must be permitted as well (for example, carrying the sacrifice to the Temple).He based his ruling on *Bemidbar* 28:2 which requires a sacrifice to be offered "at its time". Akiva objected to his teacher's ruling. Though Rabbi Eliezer had arrived at his conclusion by logical deduction, Rabbi Akiva used different logic: those activities which could be concluded before *Shabbat* must not be performed on *Shabbat*. Only the sacrifice itself was to be offered "at its time", minimizing the interference with the sanctity of *Shabbat*.

The *Mishnah* preserves the exchange between the two scholars. Rabbi Eliezer refers to his student as "Akiva", while Akiva respectfully calls his teacher "Rabbi". Rabbi Eliezer accuses his student of uprooting the Torah with his reasoning, but Rabbi Akiva manages not only to refute his teacher but to convince him. Yet, Akiva argued so respectfully that he did not alienate Rabbi Eliezer. Indeed, they admired and respected each other more and more as time went on.

For the first of many times, Rabbi Akiva's method of close examination of every word of Torah was used more convincingly than the method of applying general principles to make logical deductions. Akiva managed to redefine the interpretation of the law, opening new possibilities for creativity in specific cases. His scholarship and personable nature made him very popular with his colleagues, and he rose in prominence.

Only two of the rabbis seemed to dislike him. Elisha ben Avuyah, a fellow student, may have been mocking Rabbi Akiva when he taught that a person who learns when he is older is like words written on blotted and stained paper (*Avot* 4:20 or 25 depending on the edition). Rabban Gamliel, the head of the Yavneh academy, often had him punished for his arguing (*Arakhin* 16b), especially when Akiva rejected Rabban Gamliel's views in favor of a majority opinion. He left Yavneh for a while, but returned when the other scholars realized how much he was missed. Perhaps he learned the importance of showing deference to officials: he made a point of endorsing the ruling of Rabban Gamliel against the opinion of his teacher Rabbi Yehoshua with the words, "whatever Rabban Gamliel has done must be accepted."

Though he never held the leadership position at Yavneh, he was nonetheless a very important figure. He mediated a number of disputes and was often chosen to break difficult news to his colleagues. His outstanding compassion led him to be in charge of the distribution of aid to the poor and to care for those who were disabled — perhaps a reflection of his own beginnings.

(*Nedarim* 40a)

It happened that one of Rabbi Akiva's students took sick, but none of the sages went to visit him. Rabbi Akiva,	מעשה בתלמיד אחד מתלמידי ר' עקיבא שחלה לא נכנסו

however, went to visit him. Because he swept[1] and sprinkled[2] [the floor]* for him, he recovered. [The student] said, "Rabbi, you have given me life!" Rabbi Akiva came out and taught, "Those who do not visit a sick person may just as well have spilled his blood."

חכמים לבקרו ונכנס ר' עקיבא לבקרו ובשביל שכיבדו וריצבו לפניו חיה א"ל רבי החייתני יצא ר' עקיבא ודרש כל מי שאין מבקר חולים כאילו שופך דמים.

It might therefore come as something of a surprise that when his own son took sick, Rabbi Akiva did not leave the study hall. Rather, he sent messengers to keep track of his son's condition. As they reported worsening conditions, Akiva stuck to his studies. When a messenger finally came and told him that his son had died, he removed his *tefillin*, tore his garment and said, "To this point we were obligated to Torah; from now on we are obligated to honor the dead."

Akiva's single minded devotion to Torah came at the expense of what most people would consider to be proper dedication to family. What do you think of his decision? Can you defend the opposite point of view?

The eulogy he delivered at his son's funeral indicated the exceeding humility of Akiva and the values he sought to teach, even in the midst of his grief.

(*S'machot* 8)

Fellow Jews, listen to me. [You   אחינו ישראל שמעו

---

1) The Hebrew word kibeid also means "honored."

2) The Hebrew word ribeitz also means "taught Torah."

* Rabbi Akiva cleaned his house and sprinkled water on the dirt floor to keep the dust down.

gathered in such large numbers] not because I am a sage, for there are sages greater than I here; not because I am wealthy, for there are those wealthier than I. The people of the south know Rabbi Akiva, but how could the people of the north? The men know Rabbi Akiva, but how could the women and children? If it is because of Akiva you came — how many Akivas there are in the marketplace! Rather, I know that you only troubled yourselves to come for the sake of the *mitzvah* and to honor the Torah, saying "his God's Torah was in his heart." Therefore your reward is great, and I am comforted [and would be] had I buried seven children!

לא שאני חכם ויש כאן חכמים ממני לא שאני עשיר ויש עשירים ממני אנשי דרום מכירין את ר' עקיבא, אנשי גליל מאין מכירין. האנשים מכירין את ר' עקיבא, הנשים והטף מאין. אלא יודע אני ששכרכם מרובה שלא נצטערתם ובאתם אלא לכבוד תורה ולשם מצוה. מנחם אני שאילו היה לי שבעה בנים קברתים.

Torah was indeed the guiding force in Akiva's life. As mentioned above, it was he who developed the system for organizing the interpretations of Jewish law and lore. Before his organization, Jewish law had not been arranged by subject matter, making it very difficult to determine how to apply the principles of Torah in given situations. Rabbi Akiva took the important decisions and eliminated much of the extra and unnecessary explanations to create easily memorized texts (remember, there were few books at the time). So important a development was this that the sages credited him with saving Torah from being completely forgotten.

His appetite for learning was insatiable and his ability to absorb, interpret and teach was without equal. In fact, his friend Ben Azzai said that compared to Rabbi Akiva, the other sages had as much depth of understanding as a garlic peel!

In the midst of his growth as a scholar, news reached the Jews that the Roman government was about to impose new harsh restrictions on the Jews. Akiva and three other rabbis — Gamliel, Yehoshua and Elazar ben Azariah — sailed to Rome to plead with the Emperor for tolerance. As luck would have it, the emperor Domitian died while the rabbis were on their diplomatic mission, and his successor, Nerva, promised a more conciliatory policy. The men returned heroes, and Akiva especially was hailed as a great leader and diplomat. It seemed that his guiding philosophy of life — "whatever the Holy One does is for the good" — was justified.

Akiva founded his own school in the town of B'nai B'rak, where he lived. There he taught and often acted as judge in legal cases. Through his teaching and rulings, he expressed his belief that the law should be used whenever possible to create a balance in place of social inequalities. He taught that "all of Israel are the children of royalty," not to suggest that Jews were somehow better than others, but that no Jew was better than any other in the eyes of the law, no matter what his wealth, status or office.

One good example is his ruling that when witnesses attest to the death of a husband, they are not to be too closely examined, lest fault be found with their testimony. Were there flaws found in their testimony, the widow would be an *agunah*, that is, a woman still technically married because no court had declared her husband dead and neither had she been divorced. Akiva's ruling of selective enforcement helped to resolve the disadvantage to women of not being able to initiate a divorce under Jewish law. There were similar rulings of his which further eased the plight of women, poor people and others whose circumstances made them less-than-equal under societal conditions.

During the later years of Rabbi Akiva's life, he had one more opportunity to assert his status as a leader. After his visit to Rome, life had steadily improved for the Jews. Those who had grown up with Roman occupation seemed to adjust to it, and the Romans themselves were somewhat less occupied with crushing the Jews once Jerusalem was destroyed. However, some leaders, including Rabbi Shim'on and Rabbi Yishmael, began to teach about Jewish independence, and their nationalism gained a following. A series of edicts were issued by Rome, starting with a prohibition of circumcision and culminating in the prohibition of teaching Torah in public, which were designed to stop the nationalists.

In the course of five years, the situation deteriorated, and many sages were tempted to leave their homeland for the diaspora where they could, at least, observe the law. The teachings of Rabbi Akiva became urgently relevant.

(ADRN Ch. 26)

[Rabbi Akiva said:] Do not leave the Holy Land lest you worship idols, for David said (1 Samuel 26:19), "For they drove me

ואל תצא חוצה לארץ שמא תעבוד עבודת כוכבים שכן דוד הוא אומר (ש"א כו) כי

out today from clinging to God's trust, saying, go serve other gods." Is it even possible that King David worshiped idols? Rather, this is what David meant: If one leaves the Land of Israel and goes into the diaspora, the verse suggests that he is already an idolater... [in fact], one who is buried in the Land of Israel, it is as if he is buried under the altar, for all of the Land of Israel is fit for the holy altar. And one who is buried under the altar, it is as if he is buried under the Throne of Glory...

גרשוני היום מהסתתפח בנחלת ה' לאמר לך עבוד אלהים אחרים וכי תעלה על דעתך שדוד המלך עובד עבודת כוכבים היה. אלא כך אמר דוד כל המניח א"י ויוצא חו"ל מעלה עליו הכתוב כאילו עובד עבודת כוכבים. כל הקבור בארץ ישראל כאילו קבור תחת המזבח. לפי שכל א"י ראויה למזבח. וכל הקבור תחת המזבח כאילו קבור תחת כסא הכבוד.

At the end of the five-year period, then-emperor Hadrian visited Israel. A delegation of Jews petitioned him to ease the persecutions. For reasons of economic necessity, Hadrian ordered Jerusalem rebuilt. However, in place of the Temple, he ordered that statues of himself be erected for worship on the site of the Holy of Holies.

Rabbi Akiva was close to ninety years old. He had always urged cooperation with government, expecting respect in return. However, the pronouncement of Hadrian seemed to have let loose the very nationalistic spirit it meant to appease, and calls for rebellion swept the land. It would be simple to suggest that Akiva was caught up in that fervor, but it is unlikely that a person of his wisdom and learning would give in to mob hysteria. Instead, he most likely examined the situation and spent hours examining his principles. What resulted was a startling series of occurrences.

(Haggadah shel Pesach)

Once Rabbi Eliezer, Rabbi Yehoshua, Rabbi Elazar ben Azariah, Rabbi Akiva and Rabbi Tarfon were gathered in B'nai B'rak, and they told of Exodus from Egypt all night until their students came and said to them, "Our Rabbis! It is time to recite the *Sh'ma* of *shacharit!*"

מַעֲשֶׂה בְּרַבִּי אֱלִיעֶזֶר וְרַבִּי יְהוֹשֻׁעַ וְרַבִּי אֶלְעָזָר בֶּן עֲזַרְיָה וְרַבִּי עֲקִיבָא וְרַבִּי טַרְפוֹן, שֶׁהָיוּ מְסֻבִּין בִּבְנֵי בְרַק, וְהָיוּ מְסַפְּרִים בִּיצִיאַת מִצְרַיִם כָּל אוֹתוֹ הַלַּיְלָה, עַד שֶׁבָּאוּ תַלְמִידֵיהֶם וְאָמְרוּ לָהֶם: רַבּוֹתֵינוּ, הִגִּיעַ זְמַן קְרִיאַת שְׁמַע שֶׁל שַׁחֲרִית.

You may be quite familiar with this story from the *haggadah*, though in this context it should strike you as somewhat unusual. First of all, gathered in B'nai B'rak were the five most impressive scholars of the generation, each a man dedicated to teaching Torah at every possible moment. Yet, their students were not included in this marathon discussion, though it is obvious students were present. Next, they were gathered at Rabbi Akiva's home, not in Yavneh, where the other four were based all year. Also, the reminder which the students bring indicates that the scholars were unaware of the daylight (and therefore hiding) or that reminder was some sort of coded message — perhaps the approach of Roman investigators.

Nobody knows exactly the solutions to these dilemmas, but some believe that these five rabbis were discussing how to respond to the increasing oppression of the Romans, or perhaps planning a rebellion. One thing is clear: in the year 132, after Rabbi Shim'on and Rabbi Yishmael were executed for preaching resistance, a new hero arose by the name of Shimon bar Kokhba. Rabbi Akiva saw in him an almost mystical power, and so much as proclaimed, "It is true that Bar Kokhba is King Messiah" (*Taaniyot* 68d).

The revolution of Bar Kokhba was eventually crushed by the Romans, and the scholars who supported it either went into exile or were imprisoned. Rabbi Akiva, however, remained free for a while and continued to teach Torah openly, in defiance of the Roman ban.

(Brakhot 61b)

The Empire once banned Jews from studying Torah. Along came Pappos ben Yehudah and found Rabbi Akiva gathering crowds in public and discussing Torah. He said to him, "Akiva! Aren't you afraid of the government?" He said to him, "I will tell you a comparable story. A fox was walking along a river bank and he saw fish swarming from place to place. He said to them, 'From what are you

תנו רבנן פעם אחת גזרה מלכות הרשעה שלא יעסקו ישראל בתורה בא פפוס בן יהודה ומצאו לרבי עקיבא שהיה מקהיל קהלות ברבים ועוסק בתורה אמר ליה עקיבא אי אתה מתירא מפני מלכות אמר לו אמשול לך משל למה הדבר דומה לשועל שהיה מהלך על גב הנהר וראה דגים שהיו

fleeing?' They said to him, 'From the nets which men have cast on us.' He said to them, 'Why not come up on the dry land, and you and I will live together, just as my ancestors and yours did.' They said to him, 'Are you the one they call the cleverest of the animals? You aren't clever — you are stupid! If we are afraid in the environment which supports our life, how much more afraid would we be in an environment in which we would be sure to die?' It is the same for us, who sit and occupy ourselves with Torah, of which the verse says, 'It is your life and the length of your days (*Devarim* 30:22).' If we were to go and ignore [Torah], how much more [afraid would we be]?''

מתקבצים ממקום למקום
אמר להם מפני מה אתם
בורחים אמרו לו מפני
רשתות שמביאין עלינו
בני אדם אמר להם
רצונכם שתעלו ליבשה
ונדור אני ואתם כשם
שדרו אבותי עם
אבותיכם אמרו לו אתה
הוא שאומרים עליך פקח
שבחיות לא פקח אתה
אלא טפש אתה ומה
במקום חיותנו אנו
מתיראין במקום מיתתנו
על אחת כמה וכמה אף
אנחנו עכשיו שאנו
יושבים ועוסקים בתורה
שכתוב בה (דברים ל) כי
הוא חייך ואורך ימיך כך
אם אנו הולכים ומבטלים
ממנה עאכ"ו.

As you might expect, Akiva was eventually arrested and jailed, well into his nineties. Even so, he was allowed regular visits from his students, and he continued to teach and judge from his cell. When the visits were also curtailed, he would shout decisions from his window to a student outside. His refusal to give up Torah resulted in the sentence of death. Tradition says that the old sage was slowly tortured to death.

When the time came for Rabbi Akiva to be executed, it was the time for reciting the Sh'ma. As they tore at his skin with iron combs, he prayed to be able to accept the yoke of heaven in love. His students said to him, "Rabbi! Even at a time such as this!" He said the them, "All my life I have been bothered by the verse '[You shall love the Lord your God...] with all you soul' (Devarim 7:5), which means even if God takes your soul from you. I said, when will I ever have the chance to uphold this commandment? And now that I have the chance, should I not uphold it?" And when he got to the word echad (one), he lengthened it so that his soul departed [as he completed the Sh'ma].

בשעה שהוציאו את ר' עקיבא להריגה זמן קריאת שמע היה והיו סורקים את בשרו במסרקות של ברזל והיה מקבל עליו עול מלכות שמים אמרו לו תלמידיו רבינו עד כאן אמר להם כל ימי הייתי מצטער על פסוק זה בכל נפשך אפילו נוטל את נשמתך אמרתי מתי יבא לידי ואקיימנו ועכשיו שבא לידי לא אקיימנו היה מאריך באחד עד שיצתה נשמתו באחד.

There is no way to overstate the influence of Rabbi Akiva on Jewish life in his own time and in later Jewish history. His life is a textbook of Jewish principles and scholarship, and his leadership abilities may have rescued us from oblivion in the areas of study, practice, national identity and politics. Yet, he was not without his imperfections. Remember his initial scorn for scholars and what they represented, and his declaration that Bar Kokhba was the Messiah.

These two incidents happened at opposite ends of his life, and there were other mistakes in between. In each case, he had to admit that he was wrong, but in each case his mistakes gave him a greater insight which he put to good use.

You may find many of Akiva's leadership qualities to be the same as Rabban Yochanan ben Zakkai's. They lived in the same general period of history and faced many of the same challenges. However, many of their circumstances were different, and they were undoubtedly two very distinct kinds of people. Once again, see which traits you can identify as characteristics of Akiva's leadership, and compare them to our previous leaders.

1) Rabbi Akiva was "one of the people". Any leader must establish him- or herself with followers. It is helpful if the people see the leader as being one of their number. Rabbi Akiva's humble beginnings and inspirational triumph over ignorance in middle age gave him the kind of grass-roots support which made him all the more effective.

2) He was not afraid to challenge established systems, though he always respected them. Whether it was the initiation of his studies at a late age, the adoption of Nachum of Gamzo's method of interpretation, the visit to Rome to petition the Emperor or the endorsement of Bar Kokhba, Akiva tested the boundaries of accepted practice. At the same time, he never dismissed the system — even when he challenged the Roman government in later life, it was specific decrees he disputed, not the authority of the Emperor.

3) His strength of influence was tempered by his compassion and modesty. Remember that Rabbi Akiva never held any high office at Yavneh nor in government of any kind. He was not above taking

time from his official duties to visit a sick student. Perhaps his avoidance of official recognition gave him more credibility with his followers.

4) He was exceptionally principled and expected others to be the same. A leader must be consistent, to the point of being a paradigm or role model, if his or her leadership is to continue. Rabbi Akiva lived his life by Torah and even died by Torah, and insisted on no less from others. His appeals to the Roman authorities may have been so successful because he appealed to them on the basis of their own principles. Only when they failed to respect the Jews' values in return did Akiva rebel.

5) He could evaluate a difficult situation and find a satisfying response. Quite often, as you recall, Akiva was the mediator or the bearer of bad news because of his talent for finding the right way to respond to a situation. The eulogy for his son calmed and comforted a crowd of mourners. One can only imagine the advice he offered at the all night *seder!* Because of his consistency and credibility, he could on occasion abruptly change his tactic and not be seen as rash or unwise. His endorsement of Bar Kokhba was uncharacteristic, but accepted because of his reputation for being right.

6) Rabbi Akiva was willing to sacrifice his personal life for his career. The words of his eulogy for his son indicate that he put aside his own feelings to act the part of the leader. This was not the first, nor the last time he did so. Tradition states that he separated from his beloved wife Rachel for many years at a time to pursue his studies. When safety and prosperity could be found in Babylonia, Akiva sacrificed his security to remain in the Holy Land. In the end, he even sacrificed his life for the sake of the teaching of Torah. Not all leaders lead "extraor-

dinary" lives of personal sacrifice, but few live the "normal" lives about which they may even teach!

7) Rabbi Akiva was willing to admit his mistakes. A leader who believes that he or she is always right is eventually wrong and loses the opportunities which human imperfection create to learn from mistakes. Akiva understood that a leader who can see his faults is strengthened, not weakened, by that knowledge.

RABBAN YOCHANAN BEN ZAKKAI AND RABBI AKIVA AS PERSONAL ROLE MODELS

How can the lives and stories of these two sages and leaders give us a deeper understanding of the world around us? As before, with David and Deborah, it would be worthwhile to return to the lists of leadership traits of the two rabbis and ask some important questions:

1) What aspects of the leadership of these two men were particular to their day and age, and what aspects are not dependent on unique circumstances? How would you translate the characteristics into a modern context?

2) Certainly there were many, many rabbis who had many of the good qualities of Yochanan ben Zakkai and Akiva. There were, in all likelihood, quite a few people who were not rabbis who shared those qualities. What made these two stand out in the crowd? Why would anyone — then or now — wish to imitate the characteristics of these leaders, especially if they themselves were not leaders?

3) Are all of the leadership qualities really desirable? Would these (or other) leaders have been so effective without the less-desirable qualities? Are there

other traits, including those of David or Deborah, or those outlined by Ben Zoma or Maimonides, which could have made Akiva and Yochanan ben Zakkai better leaders — or more "Jewish" in their leadership?

*Hebrew inscription in wreath: Shimon (another name for Bar Kochba).

Chapter 5

TWO RABBINIC HEROES

BAR KOKHBA AND KETIA BAR SHALOM

This chapter will introduce two controversial heroes. Bar Kokhba led a revolt against Roman oppression about sixty years after the destruction of the Temple. Ketia bar Shalom demonstrated a brand of heroism much different from Bar Kokhba, Judah, Rachav — or indeed any common understanding of heroism.

Remember the questions from Chapter 3, which you should ask again as you learn about these two men:

1) Did he act in the best interests of the community? Who benefited from his heroic actions? Did anyone suffer for his heroism? If so, was the action worth the suffering?

2) Would you have recommended the same course of action if Bar Kokhba or Ketia bar Shalom had sought your advice?

3) Were there Jewish values expressed through this heroism? Were there Jewish values violated?

You may even find yourself asking this question about each of these people:

Were they really heroes?

BAR KOKHBA

In times of oppression and desperation, people look for someone to inspire them to overcome their situation. The more distressed people feel, the more they seek someone to offer them salvation, that is, to save them. As we already discovered in studying Rabbi Akiva's life and times, the period beginning about sixty years after the destruction of the Temple was such a time of oppression. The yoke of Roman occupation was difficult to bear under the best of circumstances for those who believed in Jewish independence, but some were able to find comfort in the study and practice of Torah. When Romans proposed a pagan temple on the site of the Holy Temple and outlawed the teaching of Torah and other important rituals, the frustrations of the people exploded.

In the year 132, after the execution of Rabbi Shim'on and Rabbi Yishmael, who had led the resistance to Rome, a man by the name of Shim'on bar Kosiba became the figure around whom the Jews rallied. Very little is known about him aside from the events of the following three years. In fact, historians had to piece together the story of his career from brief references in the Talmud and other documents of the day. In recent years, archaeological discoveries have confirmed much of what was once just theory. He was likely from the town of Kosiba in Palestine (hence, his name). He was a powerful fighter, and inspiring speaker, a brilliant strategist and a fierce believer in Jewish independence. In the small towns of Judea surrounding Jerusalem, he led bands of fighters who fortified those towns with underground passageways and stolen weapons and then attacked the Roman legions stationed in the area. So successful was he in the early part of the revolt that Jews from far-flung diaspora communities and even non-Jews unhappy with Roman governance came in droves to fight at his side.

Rabbi Akiva was among those who had concluded that the time for active resistance had arrived. The early success of Bar Kosiba led him to declare that he was the promised Messiah, Star *(Kokhav)* of Jacob. Hence, he became known as Bar Kokhba, the Aramaic translation of *ben kokhav*. Rabbi Akiva had provided the religious (and, perhaps, the intellectual) reasoning for the revolt. Bar Kokhba provided the military and political leadership.

This much historians seem to know about Bar Kokhba: he was single-minded and uncompromising in his mission to drive out Rome and restore the Jewish state. He demanded tests of loyalty and strength from his soldiers, some of whom would cut off a finger to prove their courage to him. He was known to execute those who refused to fight along side of him. At a time when a vision of overthrowing Rome altogether would have found willing and able allies in many lands, he concentrated entirely to recapturing and restoring Jerusalem and its surrounding cities to Jewish control.

At the peak of his influence, he restored sacrifices (though, obviously, not the Temple) to Jerusalem under the supervision of his close ally, Elazar the High Priest. As a sign of defiance of Rome, he ordered coins minted with his name on them: *Shim'on Nesi Yisrael* (Shim'on, Prince of Israel). He willingly accepted the title Messiah, and had the audacity to pray publicly, "Lord, if you do not help us, at least do not help our enemies; then we shall not be defeated." His prayer suggested that God needed not be a part of the military triumph.

The Roman legions in Palestine were unable to contain the revolt. Extra troops were called in from all over Europe and Asia to fight what the Romans estimated were over half a million soldiers in Bar Kokhba's army. In fact, Rome's greatest general, Julius Severus, was called in from his conquest of Britain to direct the war against the rebels.

One by one the Jewish fortresses fell, not because of superior Roman military power, but because Severus laid siege to each stronghold by cutting off food and water. There were at least seventy-five Jewish communities under independent rule at the peak of Bar Kokhba's influence. In the end, they all vanished, including Jerusalem, except for one: Betar. The siege of Betar began less than two years after the revolt began.

Every refugee of the revolt made his or her way to the stronghold south of Jerusalem. Through the cooperation of the Samaritans, whose Jewishness had always been challenged by the Jews, food and water were smuggled into the last fortress. Eventually, the Romans persuaded the Samaritans to cease their support, and Bar Kokhba became enraged at their betrayal. After almost a year and a half of fierce fighting and siege, Julius Severus sent a Samaritan spy into Betar. He sought out Elazar the Priest, who was deep in prayer, and pretended to whisper in his ear. When the incident was reported to Bar Kokhba, he demanded the Samaritan tell him what he had told Elazar. The Samaritan refused. In a fit of rage, Bar Kokhba accused Elazar of conspiracy against him and killed him. The act so demoralized the fighters that, in the year 135, the legions were able to penetrate Betar, where they slaughtered everyone.

Roman historians recorded the death toll at Betar alone to be 580,000. And yet, the passion of Bar

Kokhba and his stand at Betar provided the inspiration for Jewish resistance to oppression and national independence for centuries to come, through our own time.

There is no question that Bar Kokhba fits the macho definition of hero with which we are all familiar, but his actions certainly make him the polar opposite of Ben Zoma's prescription for heroism — he most certainly did not control his passions. Without the ill-fated revolt under his leadership, Jewish life in the Holy Land might have continued much as it had before, bearing the brunt of changes in Roman policy from better to worse and back again. Close to a million Jews died in a three-year period, and the Jewish population of Palestine was decimated because so much of the remaining population moved into exile. The surviving rabbis made Bar Kokhba a target of derision, suggesting his name "Kosiba" was derived from the word for "liar," and deeming the coins he minted as an expression of Jewish autonomy worthless.

Yet, for a brief and glorious moment in time, the powerlessness of the Jews was shattered, and an example of pride and action was set for every generation to come. Instead of passively submitting to restrictions on their sacred way of life and their mandate to serve God, the Jews took matters into their own hands and brought the most powerful empire on the face of the earth virtually to its knees for close to three years.

KETIA BAR SHALOM

Just as Bar Kokhba was not his real name, Ketia bar Shalom is most likely a pseudonym. During the reign of the Roman Emperor Domitian a generation after the destruction of the Temple, a discussion was held in the Emperor's palace about eliminating the Jews. The story below appears in the Talmud as the only record of the incident. One historian, Heinrich Graetz, suggests that Ketia bar Shalom was the nephew of the Emperor, Flavius Clemens. He may have been just one of the Emperor's advisors. No matter who he really was, he became known by his Jewish name.

(Avodah Zara 10b)

Once there was a Caesar (emperor) who hated the Jews. He said to the important members of the government, "If one had a sore on his foot[1], should he cut it off and go on with life or leave it there and suffer pain?" They said to him, "Cut it off and go on with life!" Ketia bar Shalom said to them, "First of all, you can't [eliminate] all of them, for it is written 'For as the four winds of heaven have I dispersed you (Zechariah 2:10).' If it meant that they would live dispersed in the four [corners of the earth], then instead of *as the four winds* it would have said *to the four winds*! Rather, just as the world could not exist

דההוא קיסרא דהוה סני ליהודאי אמר להו לחשיבי דמלכותא מי שעלה לו נימא ברגלו יקטענה ויחיה או יניחנה ויצטער אמרו לו יקטענה ויחיה אמר להו קטיעה בר שלום חדא דלא יכלת להו לכולהו דכתיב (זכריה ב) כי כארבע רוחות השמים פרשתי אתכם מאי קאמר אלימא דבדרתהון בד' רוחות האי כארבע רוחות לארבע רוחות מבעי ליה אלא כשם שאי אפשר לעולם בלא

---

1) The "sore" is the Jews.

without the four winds, so, too, could the world not exist without Israel. And not only that, but yours would be called a cut-off *(ketia)* kingdom!" [The Emperor] said to him, "You spoke well, however, he who bests the King [in an argument] gets thrown into a furnace." As they grabbed him and took him away, a Roman matron said to him, "Woe to the ship which sails without paying the tax[2]!" He fell on his foreskin and cut it off *(keta'a)* and said, "[When] you pay the tax, you may pass and cross over[3]." When they threw him [into the furnace] he said, "All my belongings go to Rabbi Akiva and his friends..." A voice from heaven came out and said, "Ketia bar Shalom has been invited to life in the world to come." [Then] Rabbi wept and said, "Some acquire eternal life in one hour and some eternal life after many years."

רוחות כך אי אפשר לעולם בלא ישראל ועוד קרו לך מלכותא קטיעה אמר ליה מימר שפיר קאמרת מיהו כל דזכי למלכא שדו ליה לקמוניא חלילא כד הוה נקטין ליה ואזלין אמרה ליה ההיא מטרוניתא ווי ליה לאילפא דאזלא בלא מכסא נפל על רישא דעורלתיה קטעה אמר יהבית מכסי חלפית ועברית כי קא שדו ליה אמר כל נכסאי לר' עקיבא וחביריו... יצתה בת קול ואמרה קטיעה בר שלום מזומן לחיי העולם הבא. בכה רבי ואמר יש קונה עולמו בשעה אחת ויש קונה עולמו בכמה שנים.

Ketia bar Shalom's name represents his final actions. "Ketia" means "cut-off," probably a reference

2) Roman ships had to pay a tax when they came to harbor or they were denied entry.

3) Ketia could now enter heaven as a Jew — the words for "cross over" and "Hebrew" are the same.

to his circumcision. "Bar Shalom" means "son of peace," indicating that he was at peace as a result of his act of heroism on behalf of the Jews.

What was the nature of Ketia's heroism? By standing up for what he believed, he was executed. Though he may have postponed Domitian's plans to eradicate the Jewish population of the Roman Empire, eventually Jewish life was crushed in Israel.

Ketia may have won more of a symbolic victory than an actual triumph. The story of his defiance of the Emperor had to inspire admiration and courage among the Jews. His endorsement of Rabbi Akiva, whose popularity was steadily increasing, made him more credible in the eyes of the people.

But Ketia's story had significance beyond the simple facts. Remember that the Romans constantly disparaged Jewish ritual practice, including *brit milah*, which was, then as now, the sign of God's eternal covenant with the Jews. Domitian wishes to "cut off" the sore on his foot — the Jews. Ketia suggests that he would merely cripple himself in the act. But the "cutting-off" of the foreskin, which the Romans viewed as mutilation, was far from a crippling action. Rather, it enabled Ketia and every male Jew to elevate their lives to greater holiness.

Does this story with all of its remarkable coincidences seem a little too convenient? Perhaps Ketia bar Shalom — or whoever he really was — was simply a clever Roman whose respect for the Jews carried him too far with his superiors. Perhaps as his story was told and retold, the details were embellished to make more of the story than it really was.

What is the purpose of embellishing the lives of heroes? It is a question worth discussing, because examples abound, from Choni the Circle-Maker to Herschel Ostropolier, from Paul Bunyon to Johnny Appleseed.

BAR KOKHBA AND KETIA BAR SHALOM AS PERSONAL ROLE MODELS

In discussing Judah and Rachav, it was apparent that our own times are much different than theirs. In many respects, the same can be said about Bar Kokhba and Ketia bar Shalom. Yet, there have been occasions in our own recent history which have called for role models like Bar Kokhba, and in some countries disagreeing with authorities as Ketia did could result in similar punishment. Perhaps these questions will stimulate thought and discussion on the relevance of these two heroes to our lives today.

1) Is it heroic to put values and principles before human life? At what point does the sacrifice become too great? Bar Kokhba essentially sacrificed a million souls in pursuit of a national vision of independence. Ketia sacrificed himself for the benefit of the people he adopted as his own. In each case, the victory was temporary, but the inspiration lived on.

2) In chapter 3 we asked whether a hero must act out of a sense of "rightness," or if we can separate the motives of the person from the benefits of his or her actions. Now we must turn that question inside-out. Can a person's sense of "rightness" justify actions which we might otherwise find objectionable or even immoral? In other words, in some situations, do the ends justify the means? Bar Kokhba capitalized on popular fervor to fight a war which was opposed by many on principle. Ketia bar Shalom remained a member of the Roman government, with all of its expectations of loyalty, when he apparently had deep affection for (and even secret loyalty to) the Jews, identified as enemies of the Emperor. Each justified his actions on the basis of the ends which they considered "right."

3) Especially in the case of Bar Kokhba we are faced with a modern dilemma. Like the Maccabees before him, the war he waged was essentially a guerilla war, striking at the Romans unexpectedly and terrorizing their troops in the field. Anything Roman was a target, and his destruction of Roman life and property was usual. Was Bar Kokhba a terrorist? If he was, can we truly admire him? If he was not, what distinction can be made between Bar Kokhba and terrorists?

4) Ketia bar Shalom performed his heroic actions when he was not a Jew. Would he be as much of a hero had he been Jewish at the time of his challenge to Domitian? Would he be as much of a hero to us had he not become a Jew? Would he have been a hero at all if the Emperor had not admitted to being bested in the argument, but had just put him to death for disloyalty? Is the essence of heroism in the effort or in the result?

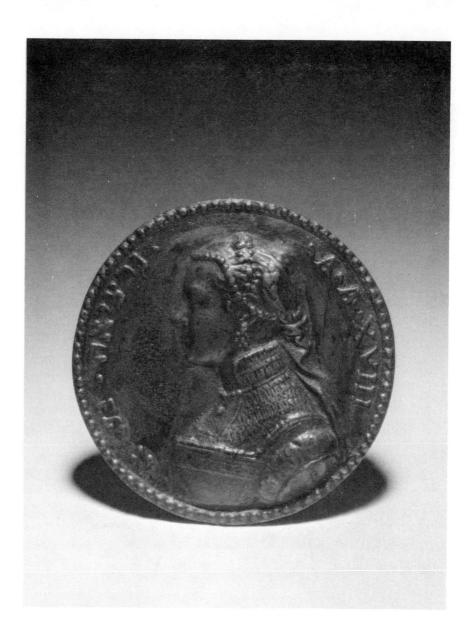

*Medal of Dona Grazia Mendes Nasi.

Chapter 6

TWO MEDIEVAL LEADERS

HASDAI IBN SHAPRUT AND DONA GRAZIA MENDES NASI

In both Biblical and Rabbinic times, the Jews enjoyed a certain amount of natural independence. Whether they were building a nation or trying to preserve it, they had strong and direct ties to the land of Israel and to however large or small a Jewish community was living there. As the lands to which the Jews were dispersed increased, the Jewish communities in those lands found themselves more and more reliant on their own resources and on relations with the native ruling powers. Different kinds of leaders and heroes emerged who were able to respond to those changes.

The medieval period in history extends approximately from the year 500 to 1500. As you know from your studies of general history, it was an era of great upheaval in Europe and Asia, encompassing terrible times of plague, impassioned grass-roots military actions like the Crusades, the growth in size and power of the Catholic Church and exceptional accomplishments, like the Magna Carta and the beginnings of the Renaissance. During this time in history, some individuals held tremendous power by virtue of their wealth or position, and could directly effect the lives of their subjects or servants. People were organized into communities identified by their role in society: peasants, warriors, merchants, craftsmen, churchmen, nobles, and so on, and were ruled by a powerful lord or king. It was virtually impossible to change one's membership in one community to another, unlike our world today.

To both our advantage and disadvantage, all Jews were members of one community, whether merchant, farmer, rabbi or physician. With our own courts, laws, customs, dress, ghettos and, of course, religion, we had an unusual amount of control over our daily lives and were able to maintain a distinct identity in the Moslem and Catholic countries in which we lived. Jews were declared a "protected minority" in these countries, subject to high levels of taxation for that privilege and in constant danger of expulsion or massacre at the whim of the ruler. Jewish community leaders learned to tread carefully in their dealings with these lords and kings, balancing the needs of their communities for practical decision-making with maintaining good will from the outside.

In some countries with a higher level of tolerance for minorities, the most highly skilled of these Jewish leaders were called to the service of the rulers they served. Their appointments presented them with unique opportunities to serve the Jews as well. Hasdai ibn Shaprut was just such a man in Moslem Spain; Dona Grazia Mendes Nasi's extraordinary career was lived in Christian Europe.

HASDAI IBN SHAPRUT
LIFE AND TIMES

Hasdai ibn Shaprut ("ibn" is Arabic for "ben," or "son of") was born into a wealthy family in the south of Spain around the year 915 CE. When he was a young man his family moved to Cordoba, the capital of Moslem Spain. Cordoba was at that time one of the most important cities in the world, boasting a blend of government and culture often found in medieval Moslem cultures. Though overwhelmingly Moslem in population, the tolerant government allowed for free interaction with Jews and Christians, and even employed them. Literature, science and philosophy flourished in an atmosphere of mutual respect.

The Jewish community of Cordoba was close to a hundred years old when Hasdai arrived, and relatively well established. Shortly after his arrival, Hasdai began medical studies and entered the service of the Moslem Caliph (ruler), Abd al-Rahman III. During that time, a diplomatic delegation arrived from Byzantium (the remnant of the Eastern Roman Empire) and brought with it a gift for the Caliph: an ancient Greek medical text on drugs. Hasdai was part of the group which translated it into Arabic, impressing the Caliph with his mastery of languages. As a reward, the Caliph promoted him to a high-level position in the government; he was put in charge of collecting taxes on imports (customs), a position called "vizir." Hasdai was 29 years old.

HIS CAREER AS A LEADER

Hasdai's talents as linguist, diplomat and government official placed him in more and more international negotiations on behalf of the Caliph, including a successful mission to the Christian Spanish kingdom of Leon, which deposed its obese ruler, Sancho. Ironically, it was a combination of this mission and his medical skills which provided him with his greatest diplomatic triumph. Sent by the Caliph to Navarre, another Christian kingdom in Spain, Hasdai was asked by their Queen Tota to help her grandson, none other than the deposed ruler of Leon, to lose weight. Whatever diet he prescribed (which is, unfortunately, lost to history) worked, and a grateful Queen Tota agreed to a treaty with Cordoba which would ensure Sancho a return to his own kingdom of Leon!

Tota and Sancho even agreed to return with Hadsai to Cordoba for ceremonies finalizing the treaty. The arrival of two Christian rulers in the capital of Moslem Spain was a diplomatic event without equal, and Hasdai was rewarded by the Caliph with another governmental promotion including the title of head of the Jewish community of Moslem Spain. The extent of his power within the government is apparent from a letter Hasdai wrote to Joseph, King of the Khazars:

> Our king has collected very large treasures of silver, gold, precious things and valuables such as no king has ever collected. His yearly revenue is about 100,000 gold pieces, the greater part of which is derived from merchants who come hither from various countries and islands; all their mercantile transactions are placed under my control... Kings of the earth... bring gifts to [the Caliph]... All their gifts pass through my hands, and I am charged with making gifts in return.

Hasdai's influence in the Jewish community was equally powerful. The Jews in Spain had relied on rabbis in Babylonia for religious guidance. Hasdai appointed an Italian refugee scholar, Moses ben Hanokh, as chief rabbi of Cordoba, and Moses's efforts created an independent rabbinical authority in Spain. When Moses died, many in the community wanted to replace him with a more worldly man, educated in the secular knowledge of the time. Hasdai insisted on appointing Moses's son Hanokh instead, a rabbi renown for his piety and scholarship, but less educated in secular matters.

As mentioned above, the medieval Moslem culture was intertwined with government, and government officials often used their influence and wealth to support the arts. Hasdai became a patron (financial supporter) to poets and other writers of the Jewish community, sponsoring Menachem ibn Saruq (who wrote an important Hebrew dictionary and grammar) and Dunash ibn Labrat (who composed the Shabbat hymn D'ror Yikra). It should be noted that Hasdai was not very generous in his support, often maintaining the poets in near-poverty. Nonetheless, the artists he sponsored left us many magnificent poems dedicated to Hasdai, and his interest in Hebrew literature began a "golden age" of such writing in Spain. Two hundred years later, the Spanish Jewish historian Abraham ibn Da'ud proclaimed: *

In the days of Rabbi Hasdai the Prince, the bards began to twitter...

Hasdai was concerned not only with the Jews of his community, but with Jews abroad as well. When he heard that Jews were being persecuted in the

*Sefer Ha-Qabbalah, p. 102

Byzantine empire of Empress Helena, he wrote to her politely asking that the Jews be granted the freedom to practice their religion. However, he included the thinly veiled threat that to this point the Christians of Spain had not been persecuted by him. His power and his absolute loyalty to his people led him to write in a letter to King Joseph:

> When God saw [Spanish Jewry's] misery and labor, and that they were helpless, he led me to present myself before the Caliph, and has graciously turned His heart to me, not because of mine own righteousness, but for His mercy and His covenant's sake... I always ask the ambassadors about our brethren the Israelites, the remnant of the captivity, whether they have heard anything concerning the deliverance of those who have pined in bondage and had found no rest.

The letter to Joseph already mentioned twice is the document which has given Hasdai his greatest reputation among the Jews. Joseph was king of Khazaria, a kingdom located on the Caspian Sea in an area that is now part of the Soviet Union. The Khazars were of the same ethnic background as the Turks, but they were not conquered by the Moslems, and so maintained their own identity. In the year 740, the ruler of Khazaria and most of its people converted to Judaism, creating a Jewish kingdom. As you might imagine, the event captured the interest and imagination of Jews everywhere, and many Jews saw the conversion as the beginning of a redemption which would bring the Jews back to Israel under their own leadership. Hasdai wrote:

108

We [Jews] have been cast down from our glory, so that we have nothing to reply when [the non-Jews] say daily to us, "Every other people has its kingdom, but of yours there is no memorial on the earth." Hearing, therefore, the fame of my Lord the King [of the Khazars], as well as the power of his dominions, and the multitude of his forces, we were amazed, we lifted up our head, our spirit revived and our hands were strengthened, and the kingdom of my Lord furnished us with an argument in answer to this taunt.

Hasdai wrote to Joseph in order to find out if the reports of the Khazarian kingdom were indeed true. If they were, it would strengthen Hasdai's hand in his attempts to improve the situation of the Jews in Spain. He also wanted to know if Joseph had heard anything about the coming of the Messiah, since this would end the suffering and powerlessness of the Jews in the world.

Joseph responded to Hasdai's inquiries with a long history of his people and their practices, and addressed the question about the Messiah:

Our eyes are turned to the Lord our God and to the wise men of Israel who dwell in Jerusalem and Babylon... we know aught concerning this. But if it please the Lord, he will do it for the sake of his great name...

Joseph concluded with a desire to meet Hasdai, as he had requested. For reasons lost to history, the meeting never took place.

Hasdai died in about 970.

Take a few moments to list those qualities which

made Hasdai ibn Shaprut an effective leader. How do they compare with the earlier models of Jewish leadership? How does your list compare with the list which follows?

1) Hasdai was wealthy and well-placed. Though it is certainly not a requirement for leadership, wealth and "friends in high places" quite often make the road to leadership easier to travel. You might compare Hasdai's meteoric rise to prominence with the story of Joseph in Pharoah's court for both their similarities and differences.

2) Hasdai was a well-rounded person. At a time when most people limited their expertise to the community with which they were identified, Hasdai had an extensive education and skill in medicine, language, business, cultural arts and certainly many other things. His ability to meet people on their own terms, whether the Caliph, Queen Tota or his own people, made him a much more effective leader.

3) Hasdai had a knack for being in the right place at the right time. We often attribute such a knack to coincidence, but Hasdai seems to have been able to evaluate circumstances and "create coincidence." For example, he used his appointment as head of the Jewish community and his position in the Spanish government to deliver a message about the treatment of the Jews to Empress Helena.

4) Like David, Hasdai was exceptionally loyal. Throughout the period of his service to the Caliph, there appears to be no inference that he had conflicting loyalties to Spain and to the Jews. Indeed, he had *dual loyalties*, but he seemed able to balance his various roles to everyone's admiration.

5) Hasdai was devoted to Jewish integrity. Concerned about the physical and cultural distance between Spain and Babylonia, he took decisive action

to ensure the flourishing of Judaism in Spain by the appointment of a Chief Rabbi. It may be that his dedication to Hanokh ben Moses succeeding his father was for precisely the reason that Hanokh was less wordly than his rival — Hasdai sought to preserve a certain distance between Judaism and the host culture of Spain.

6) Hasdai used the powers of governmental office to the benefit of his people. Were it not for Hasdai's influence, he would not have been able to support the works of ibn Labrat and ibn Saruq. Were it not for his prestige in Spain, his concern for the plight of Byzatium's Jews might have been an empty gesture. You might compare Hasdai's efforts to those of other prominent Jews in national governments: Benjamin Disraeli in Great Britain, Henry Kissinger in the United States, Leon Trotsky in the USSR.

7) He knew the power of compromise and coalition politics. As a diplomat, Hasdai knew that one usually cannot get something without giving in return. The peace treaty with Tota came as a result of the pledge to return Sancho to his throne. The relief for Jews in Helena's empire came as the result of an implied promise to protect his interests in Cordoba. Hasdai did not demand his way without seeing the other party's interests.

DONA GRAZIA MENDES NASI

LIFE AND TIMES

In the centuries following Hasdai's death, the Jews of Spain suffered many changes in fortune. When the Christians overthrew the Moslem rulers of Spain, the relative freedom which the Jews had enjoyed ended, and the very conditions Hasdai had sought to relieve in Byzantium were imposed to a greater and greater extent on his own descendants. By 1492, the Jews of Spain were given an ultimatum by King Ferdinand and Queen Isabella: convert to Catholicism or leave Spain. As you might expect, most chose to leave Spain, and they dispersed to all points of the Jewish world. A large number (150,000) moved to nearby Portugal, where conditions were somewhat better. Within five years a greater horror awaited the Portugese Jewish community. They were all forcibly converted to Christianity, and by 1499 these "Conversos" ("New Christians") were prohibited from leaving Portugal, as many of them tried to do. Most of the Conversos were still practicing Judaism secretly, and if they were found out, they were persecuted or even executed.

In the year 1510, a wealthy Portuguese Converso family named Nasi was blessed with a daughter named Beatrice de Luna. Though publicly loyal to their conversion, and therefore able to succeed in their business ventures, they were privately devoted Jews and named their daughter Grazia. At age 18, Grazia married Francisco Mendes, also a Converso, a banker whose interests included a branch in Antwerp, in the Spanish Netherlands. They had one daughter, Brianda (who later changed her name to Reyna). Francisco died in 1537, and on the pretext of business, Dona (Lady) Grazia left Portugal with her daughter, her sister and her nephew. The situation for the Conversos in Portugal had become intolerable; the Inquisition was raging and "secret Jews" were being tortured and executed for disloyalty to the Church. Making her way to Antwerp, where Francisco's brother Diogo ran the family business, Grazia immersed herself in the bank and in her brother-in-law's secret work aiding Converso refugees.

Afraid of retribution, Grazia and her family continued to hide their Jewish practice. A few years after arriving in Antwerp, Diogo died and a Catholic nobleman, perhaps anxious for wealth, asked for Reyna in marriage. In 1545 Dona Grazia and her family secretly left Antwerp for Venice.

Some time during their first four years in Venice, Grazia's sister really converted, and informed on Grazia's secret practices to the authorities. She was imprisoned for her "heresy," but was released after the intervention of Diogo's widow with local authorities.

HER CAREER AS A LEADER

After Grazia's release from prison, she moved to the city of Ferrara, where the local rulers were sympathetic to refugees. There she finally threw off her Christian name of Beatrice and lived openly as a Jew. Her business acumen and survival instincts allowed her to prosper, and she used her wealth to continue the interrupted family aid to Converso refugees and to support Jewish culture. Before too long her reputation for helping those in need, whether fleeing for their lives or improving the quality of their art, made her among the most honored Jews of her time.

One indication of her importance is the dedication of the Bible published in Ferrara with a literal translation into Spanish:

Prologue to the Very Magnificent Lady: We are about to print the Bible in our Spanish tongue (translated from the Hebrew word — so rare a work never before known until our day). Therefore we desire to direct it to your

Honor, as being the person whose merits have always earned the most sublime place among our people.*

Dona Grazia also funded the work of Samuel Usque, a Converso refugee. In 1553, he wrote a work in Portuguese entitled *Consolations for the Tribulations of Israel*. This work attempted to find meaning in the sufferings of the Spanish and Portuguese Jewish communities, much as earlier *midrash* had interpreted the destructions of the Temples and later literature would plumb the horrors of the Holocaust. He dedicated the work to Grazia, calling her the "heart in the body of our people." He also wrote, "you have done more than all of [Jewish personalities] to bring forth into light the fruit of the plants that lie buried in the darkness." No doubt, Usque was referring to her efforts on behalf of the exiles from Spain and Portugal.

Grazia's efforts on behalf of the oppressed refugees found its way into Usque's book. Calling her the personification of consolation, he described many of her efforts in detail, embellishing the account with the flowery style of writing he employed.

Thus with her golden hand and majestic purpose, she lifted the majority of our people in Europe from the abyss of this hardship and countless [numbers] from where poverty and sin had hurled them. She continued to guide them until they were in safe lands, and until she had returned them to the obedience and precepts of their ancient God. Thus she has been a stay in

---

The House of Nasi: Dona Grazia p. 73

your weakness, a prop for the weary, a clear fountain for the thirsty, a shady tree, full of fruit, which has fed the hungry and sheltered the forsaken.*

As dramatic as it may sound in Usque's writing, Dona Grazia was indeed responsible for the rescue, support and rehabilitation of thousands upon thousands of Conversos, who might otherwise have been swept under the tide of official anti-Jewishness in the time of the Inquisition.

In the year *Consolations* was published, Dona Grazia moved from Ferrara to Constantinople. In this center of the Ottoman Empire, Jews enjoyed much greater freedom and religious liberty under Moslem rule. Thriving in this nurturing environment, she became a patron of scholars and devoted her considerable wealth and skills to the construction of schools, *yeshivot* and synagogues, work which was continued by her daughter and son-in-law long after she retired from public life.

The last project she undertook began in 1559. With her son-in-law, Joseph, she devoted all of her energies toward lobbying the Sultan of Turkey to allow the rebuilding of Tiberias in Israel, which was in ruins at the time. He granted her request on a temporary basis, and Joseph devoted much effort to successfully renewing the Sultan's permission. Dona Grazia endowed the building of a *yeshivah* there, and may have visited it during her declining years, perhaps even dying on such a visit to *Eretz Yisrael*.

Dona Grazia Mendes Nasi retired from public life in 1559, perhaps because of failing health. She died in 1569 and was mourned by the entire Jewish

---

Consolations for the Tribulations of Israel, p. 230

world. Of her, historian Cecil Roth wrote, "No other woman in Jewish history has been surrounded by such devotion and affection."

Now is the time to list your impressions of Dona Grazia's leadership qualities. How does her leadership compare to an "official" leader like Hasdai ibn Shaprut? Do you find similarities between Deborah and Grazia? How does your list of Grazia's leadership qualities compare to the list which follows?

1) Dona Grazia had empathy for the people. Because she knew first-hand of their suffering, Grazia was able to feel the pain of the Conversos. Rather than wallowing in despair, she translated her understanding into action.

2) She was shrewd. In the dangerous politics of medieval Europe, being educated was not enough. One had to be able to "beat the system". Dona Grazia was able to maintain the appearance of faithful convert for many years while secretly plotting to preserve and support Jewish heritage and practice. There is a certain willful dishonesty necessary for such a life to succeed. You might discuss the limits of such deceit in public life.

3) Dona Grazia was devoted to two essential Jewish values appropriate to times of trouble. The first is *pidyon shevuyim*, the ransoming of captives, and the second *piku'ach nefesh*, the saving of life. What is important about her efforts in these areas to us is that she saw them as Jewish imperatives, not simply as the "right thing to do".

4) Grazia was devoted to two essential Jewish values appropriate to Jews at all times. It is sometimes easier to be a leader in the midst of crisis because remedies seem so urgent and apparent. However, Dona Grazia was devoted to the positive, ongoing support of Jewish life through her devotion to *talmud*

torah, the study and support of Torah for herself and others, and *binyan ha'artez*, the building up of the Land of Israel.

5) She maintained a sense of hope and optimism throughout her life. As you can tell from the praise of her work by Usque and the Jews of Ferrara, Dona Grazia was not merely a patron of the Jewish community, she was an inspiration to them. Certainly she had much reason to become bitter: the death of her husband, the betrayal by her sister, the constant deception, the numerous uprootings she suffered. Nonetheless, she maintained a sense of her ability to effect *tikkun olam*, a betterment of the world around her.

HASDAI IBN SHAPRUT AND DONA GRAZIA MENDES NASI AS PERSONAL ROLE MODELS

Moreso than the earlier leaders we have studied, both Hasdai and Grazia lived in times similar to our own. Of course, we do not suffer from the tyranny of oppressive or whimsical rulers, and though Jews are often a minority, we are not dependent on the good will of an individual or group of individuals to continue our lives as Jews. Nonetheless, both of these leaders lived in societies requiring a great deal of contact with the non-Jewish population and a good deal of diplomacy in dealing with them — as in our world today.

Take a look at the leadership qualities of these two people and at the qualities of the biblical and Rabbinic leaders. How do they compare? Are any of the qualities of David or Deborah, of Rabban Yochanan or Rabbi Akiva "transferable" to Hasdai or Grazia? Would such a transfer have made either leader more or less effective? Could the earlier leaders have benefited from the experience of these medieval leaders? Most importantly, would you want to emulate the qualities of these two leaders?

1) Were Hasdai and Dona Grazia unique to their times? From the picture you have gained of their tactics and values, would they have been as effective in each other's world? How would you have advised them on the difficult decisions they had to make, for example, choosing a successor for the Chief Rabbi or dealing with a sister who had decided to reveal your deception? Would these two leaders have been effective in our world?

2) Were all of the character traits necessary to their successful leadership desirable? Knowing of Grazia's life of deceit, would she be a trustworthy leader today? Was her hiding of her true loyalties proper or merely a necessity of the times? Was Hasdai's rather shameless bragging about his powers a sign of security or of conceit? Would he have been more or less effective were he more humble?

3) How do the teachings of Ben Zoma and Maimonides from Chapter 1 relate to these two leaders?

Chapter 7

TWO MEDIEVAL HEROES

RABBI JUDAH LOEW OF PRAGUE AND RABBI MEIR OF ROTENBURG

We will now encounter two men who were seemingly larger than life, and face two issues through them which raise difficult questions about heroism. Each of these rabbis was a prominent leader in his generation, but it is not their leadership on which we focus. It is extremely worthwhile to learn more about these rabbis, the influence they had on their communities and their place in Jewish history. However, sometimes a leader becomes known for a heroic act which can overshadow his leadership.

In the case of Rabbi Meir, the act of heroism was an act of self-denial. Rabbi Meir died in prison, a martyr for his principles and the welfare of the Jewish community.

In the case of Rabbi Judah, also known as the *Maharal*, the act of heroism for which he is most remembered *never really happened*. Nonetheless, it is celebrated in the folklore of our people.

Remember the questions from Chapter 3, which you should ask again as you learn about these two men:

1) Did he act in the best interests of the community? Who benefited from his heroic actions? Did anyone suffer for his heroism? If so, was the action worth the suffering?

2) Would you have recommended the same course of action if Rabbi Judah or Rabbi Meir had sought your advice?

3) Were there Jewish values expressed through this heroism? Were there Jewish values violated?

Other questions will be raised by these acts of heroism. It will be most valuable to spend the time formulating questions about the men and their actions.

RABBI JUDAH LOEW BEN BETZALEL OF PRAGUE

At the entrance to the Jewish town hall in Prague, Czechoslovakia stands a statue of Rabbi Judah Loew (sometimes spelled "Loeb") ben Betzalel. He is so honored because in the long history of the city he is considered among its most outstanding citizens. He lived from 1525-1609, and in the course of his lifetime mastered the breadth and depth of Jewish learning, publishing volumes of interpretation, commentary and philosophy identified by his title, *Maharal mi-Prag* (an abbreviation of *moreinu ha-rav loeb*). He was a true innovator in Jewish learning, blending the mystical with the rational and emphasizing the importance of appreciating the emotional impact of Torah as much as the intellectual.

The *Maharal* was also well educated in mathematics and alchemy (the forerunner of chemistry) and a wide variety of other secular subjects. He earned respect and reputation among Jews and non-Jews alike, so much so that he was once invited to meet privately with Emperor Rudolph II of Europe and, when he became Chief Rabbi of Prague, it was a source of great pride for the city.

These brief paragraphs do not do justice to the general influence or scholarly works of Rabbi Judah Loew. He was a great leader of our people in medieval Europe. Yet, outside of students of Talmud who regularly refer to his work *Be'er HaGolah*, he is best remembered for an act of heroism which never occured.

There are, in every culture, stories of fantasy and fancy. In spite of the fact that our tradition has always officially rejected the idea of magic, there have remained superstitions among our people which impute great magical powers to those who are deeply pious, exceptionally learned and masters of the *Kabbalah* (mystic tradition). The Maharal was such a person, and so a legend which has appeared in various forms throughout Jewish history became permanently attached to him. It is the legend of the Golem, a humanoid creature made of clay whose unlimited strength is controlled only by the use of certain Hebrew names and words, and then only by those who can use those words properly.

Many versions of the Judah Loew-Golem story exist, including a novel by author Gustav Meyrink and a play by Yiddish poet H. Leivick, as well as many children's versions of the story. It appears to be based on local legends from Prague (where Meyrink did most of his research) and refers to events which did not even occur in the *Maharal's* lifetime. The version included below is a translation of the story "Der Golem," by Yiddish writer I.L.Peretz. It raises some basic questions about such heroic acts, but does not include details which Meyrink and Leivick develop in their longer works, especially the Golem turning on the Jews and the rabbi's internal struggle over the monster he created.

(Translation of *"The Golem"* from *A Treasury of Yiddish Stories*).

Great men were once capable of great miracles.

When the ghetto of Prague was being attacked, and they were about to rape the women, roast the children, and slaughter the rest; when it seemed that the end had finally come, the great Rabbi Loeb put aside his *Gemarah*, went into the street, stopped before a heap of clay in front of the teacher's house, and molded a clay image. He blew into the nose of the *golem* — and it began to stir; then he whispered the Name into its ear, and our *golem* fell upon our enemies, threshing them as with flails. Men fell on all sides.

Prague was filled with corpses. It lasted, so they say, through Wednesday and Thursday. Now it is already Friday, the clock strikes twelve, and the *golem* is still busy at its work.

"Rabbi," cries the head of the ghetto, "the *golem* is slaughtering all of Prague! There will not be a gentile left to light the Sabbath fires or take down the Sabbath lamps."

Once again the rabbi left his study. He went to the altar and began singing the psalm "A song of the Sabbath."

The *golem* ceased its slaughter. It returned to the ghetto, entered the House of

Prayer, and waited before the rabbi. And again the rabbi whispered into its ear. The eyes of the *golem* closed, the soul that had dwelt in it flew out, and it was once more a *golem* of clay.

To this day the *golem* lies hidden in the attic of the Prague synagogue, covered with cobwebs that extend from wall to wall. No living creature may look at it, particularly women in pregnancy. No one may touch the cobwebs, for whoever touches them dies. Even the oldest people no longer remember the *golem*, though the wise man Zvi, the grandson of the great Rabbi Loeb, ponders the problem: may such a *golem* be included in a congregation of worshipers or not?

The *golem*, you see, has not been forgotten. It is still here! But the Name by which it could be called to life in a day of need, the Name has disappeared. And the cobwebs grow and grow, and no one may touch them.

What are we to do?

Translated by Irving Howe

In chapter 5 we met Ketia bar Shalom, whose story may have been embellished. Now we are faced with a larger question: why would an act of heroism be invented? In answering the general question, perhaps these considerations would be worth some thought:

1) Why was a scholarly, pious and respected figure like Rabbi Judah Loew chosen for the hero of this story? Was his reputation exploited to give the story a more believable basis? Did his knowledge of mysticism lend credibility to the creation of the Golem? Was his righteousness used to excuse an

ordinarily unrighteous act? (Recall Rabbi Akiva's support of Bar Kochba).

2) Why did the rabbi create an inhuman defender instead of training and arming the Jews?

3) What reasons can you think of for the Golem going out of control? Was the loss of control the result of having no conscience, or was the Golem a reflection of the pent-up anger of the Jewish community? The rabbi had the power to control the Golem — why did he not do so until the Jews reported the Golem's excesses?

4) The head of the ghetto gave an unusual reason to stop the slaughter. Would you have found a different reason to stop the Golem? What Jewish values were expressed and what Jewish values were violated by this exchange?

5) The story concludes with a number of questions. Why is contact with the lump of clay, or even the attached cobwebs, dangerous? What do you think of the rabbi's grandson considering only the question of whether the Golem could be counted in a minyan? Why does the author emphasize the idea that the "Name" has disappeared? What is the meaning of the last line of the story?

About now you may be wondering why a fictional act of heroism was included in a source book devoted to role models. "The Golem" is about heroic power gone out of control, about creating a vehicle for defense of the Jews and their security and then finding it has exceeded its mission, about the anguish of the community in confronting the power it has unleashed.

Such situations have presented themselves to us in our own day and age. How should we respond to them? Were it not for the wisdom of Rabbi Judah Loew, says the story, there would have been no

Golem. Were it not for the Golem, there would have been no Jews in Prague.

RABBI MEIR BEN BARUKH OF ROTENBURG

Rabbi Meir, also known as *Maharam (Moreinu HaRav Meir)*, was the descendant of a long line of prominent scholars who lived in Germany. He lived from 1215-1293, during which time he became the most respected scholar and teacher in Western Europe. His commentaries on the Talmud are still widely studied (some appear along side the printed text of the *Gemara),* and he was a major influence on the authors of the *Arba'ah Turim, Mordechai, Haggahot Maimuniyot* and other collections of Jewish law, which, in turn, were the foundation for the *Shulchan Arukh,* the authoritative code of Jewish law compiled in the sixteenth century.

Until the year 1286, Rabbi Meir lived a peaceful and honored life as a respected scholar, attaining the position of Chief Rabbi of Germany, which gave him full authority to make decisions about Jewish law. He made significant contributions to the understanding of Jews about their responsibilities regarding taxes imposed by non-Jewish authorities and the right of the Jewish community to tax its members. These responsa (answers to legal questions) were ironic, because in 1286, Emperor Rudolph I of Germany imposed a new series of taxes and regulations on the Jews of Germany which effectively made them slaves.

The Jews were outraged, and with the encouragement of the *Maharam,* refused to pay the taxes and began to leave Germany in large numbers. Rabbi Meir himself decided to leave the country, and had brought his family to the port city of Lombardy in preparation for departure. An apostate Jew (one who converted away from Judaism) recognized him and informed the authorities of his plans. Rabbi Meir was arrested and delivered to the Emperor, who put him in prison.

The Emperor planned to hold Rabbi Meir for ransom. However, the ransom he desired was not just money (at one time the Jews agreed to pay a ransom of 23,000 pounds of silver!), but an agreement that he had the right to impose the taxes.

(Yam Shel Shlomo on the tractate *Gittin,* Ch. 4:66)

I have heard that the *Maharam of Rotenberg* (may his memory be for a blessing) was imprisoned in the tower of Ensisheim for a number of years. The government official demanded a great sum [for ransom] from the [Jewish] communities. The communities wanted to redeem him, but he [the *Maharam*] did not allow them. He said: "One does not redeem captives for more money than they are worth." [from the *Mishnah* in *Gittin* chapter 4].

I am surprised, for since he was a great scholar, there was none other like him in his generation in stature in knowledge of Torah and in piety, it was permitted [halachically] to redeem him at any price! If he refused out of humility, that he did not wish

שמעתי על מהר"ם מרוטנבר"ק ז"ל שהיה תפוס במגדול אייגזהם כמה שנים והשר תבע מן הקהלות סך גדול והקהלות היו רוצים לפדותו ולא הניח כי אמר אין פודין השבויים יותר מכדי דמיהם. ותמה אני מאחר שהיה תלמיד חכם מופלג ולא היה כמותו בדורו בתורה ובחסידות ושרי לפדותו בכל ממון שבעולם ואם מרוב ענותנותו לא רצה להחזיק עצמו כתלמיד חכם מופלג מכל מקום היה לו לחוש על

to regard himself as a great scholar, he still should have worried about refraining from studying the Torah. He wrote that he was sitting in darkness and "the shadow of death" [Psalm 23] without Torah and light, and he was lamenting that he had no access to the legal codes and the Talmud commentators. How could he not have been concerned about the sin of refraining from study, especially since so many [of the community] needed him?

Certainly he thought that if the communities redeemed him then we should fear that all other governments would do the same to the great scholar of each generation in order to get exorbitant ransoms. [If that happened] the Diaspora [communities] would not have enough money to redeem them and, consequently, Torah would be forgotten from Israel. Therefore, the *hassid* [the *Maharam*] said that it would be better if a little extra knowledge [his own] be lost from Israel than if most of the knowledge be lost.

ביטול תורה כאשר כתב בעצמו שהוא היה יושב בחושך וצלמות בלי תורה ואורה והיה מקונן שלא היו אצלו ספרי הפוסקים והתוספות ואיך לא היה חש לעון ביטול התורה מאחר שרבים צריכים לו. ובודאי דעתו היה שאם יפדו אותו אם כן יש למיחש שלא יעשו כן כל השרים לתלמיד חכם המופלג שבדור בעבור רוב הממון עד שלא יספיק ממון הגולה לפדותם ותשתכח התורה מישראל. ומשום הכא אמר החסיד מוטב שתאבד מעט חכמה היתרת מישראל ממה שתאבד חכמת התורה עיקר.

Rabbi Meir refused to allow the Jews to redeem him under such circumstances, and died seven years later in prison. His body remained unburied for another fourteen years until it was ransomed and interred in his birthplace, the city of Worms.

It is important to note that Jews were held for ransom with great frequency in medieval Europe, the Mediterranean, and Nazi Germany; and are still in certain Arab countries and the Soviet Union.

RABBI JUDAH LOEW OF PRAGUE AND RABBI MEIR OF ROTENBURG AS PERSONAL ROLE MODELS

Perhaps you are questioning whether these last two heroes and their actions have anything to do with your own life. After all, Rabbi Judah Loew's supposed act of heroism was fiction in form and fantasy in substance. Rabbi Meir's heroism took place in a different time and under a different government that any of us, God willing, will ever know.

The issue is worth a second look, however. The examples of these two men may not now or always be quite so far removed from your life.

As you may recall from the discussion of Rabbi Akiva, he went to great lengths to promote the *mitzvah* of living in the Land of Israel. In our time, we have the privilege and opportunity to fulfill this *mitzvah* in the independent and Jewish State of Israel. One of the obligations of Israeli citizenship is service in the Israeli Defense Forces *(TZAHAL)*.

In 1982, the IDF undertook "Operation Peace for the Galilee," a military invasion of southern Lebanon designed to destroy or disable bases used for terrorist attacks against the residents of northern Israel. These orders were issued to all members of the IDF on June 11, 1982, on the eve of the operation.

(Excerpted from "Igeret LaChayal B'Levanon 11 Yuni 1982")

THE IMAGE OF THE ISRAELI SOLDIER

IDF will now be occupying a large amount of territory in Lebanon. Its soldiers will come into contact with a large and varied civilian population. This contact stands before you as a challenge to your humanity, your Jewishness and your service in IDF.

• It is expressly forbidden to take any kind of booty from any source whatsoever. Anyone who violates this order may expect to stand trial and be punished with up to ten years in prison...

• Do not disturb the peaceful civilian population, and especially do not disturb the honor of the women.

• It is the responsibility of every IDF soldier to refrain from disturbing places which house cultural artifacts, including sites of antiquities, museums, and the like.

צה"ל שוהה עתה בשטחים נרחבים בלבנון חייליו באים במגע עם אוכלוסיה אזרחית גדולה ומגוונת, מגע זה מעמיד בפניך אתגר של התנהגות אנושית, יהודית וצה"לית.

• חל איסור מוחלט לקחת ביזה מכל מקור שהוא. כל העובר על הוראה זו צפוי להעמדה לדין ולעונש מקסימלי של עשר שנות מאסר...

• אין לפגוע באוכלוסיה האזרחית השלווה, ובמיוחד אין לפגוע בכבודן של נשים.

• חובה על כל חיילי צה"ל להימנע מפגיעה במקומות בהם נמצאים נכסי תרבות, לרבות אתרי עתיקות, מוזיאונים וכד'.

• חל איסור לפגוע במקומות הקדושים לכל הדתות.

• It is expressly forbidden to disturb the holy places of any religion.

Any war stirs up feelings of hatred, vengeance and the devaluation of the enemy's life and property. As a result of these feelings, every person is responsible, because he is a human being, to preserve the principles of morality which are the basis of established human society. IDF is fighting, this time, a cruel enemy which uses, as a tactic of warfare, terror against defenseless citizens.

It is forbidden for IDF to act according to that standard which is acceptable to our enemies. It is forbidden to allow feelings of revenge to guide us in our behavior against the civilian population of Lebanon. Our uniqueness and our strength comes from preserving our humanity...

The principles of morality are based in the Jewish tradition. Even in time of war, it is worth

כל מלחמה מעוררת רגשות שנאה, נקמה וזלזול בחיים וברכוש אויב. למרות רגשות אלה חייב כל אדם באשר הוא אדם, לשמור על עקרונות מוסר, שהם הבסיס לקיומה של חברה אנושית. צה"ל נלחם הפעם באויב אכזרי, שהפעיל כשיטת לחימה, טירור כלפי אזרחים חסרי הגנה.
לצה"ל אסור לפעול לפי אותן אמות-מידה המקובלות על אויבינו; אסור שרגשות נקם ידריכו את התנהגותנו כלפי האוכלוסיה האזרחית בלבנון.
ייחודנו וכוחנו בשמירת צלם אנוש...
עקרונות מוסר הם מיסודה של המורשת היהודית. גם בעת מלחמה ראוי שנזכור כי אדם לאדם הוא — אדם

remembering that human
being to human being —
every person is a human
being.

(The orders close with an excerpt from the
seventh chapter of the book of Joshua. Achan was a
soldier who violated Joshua's prohibition against
looting the enemy. The Israelites executed him for
bringing them disgrace and lowering them in God's
eyes.)

1) Compare the story of the Golem with the
orders of the Israeli Defense Forces. Which seems to
you to be the best expression of Jewish values? If you
were faced with the opportunity to let loose a
"golem" in Lebanon (or any war) would you do so? If
you could create so powerful a weapon of defense,
which might save many Jewish lives, would you be
persuaded by the IDF orders? How does the teaching
of Ben Zoma relate to this issue?

2) Rabbi Meir's principle of restraint did not
prevent similar hostage-taking after the fact. The
overwhelmingly exemplary behavior of Israeli soldiers
in the "Operation Peace for the Galilee" did not
prevent their enemies — nor even their allies — from
sinking to a level of immoral behavior and attacks on
civilian populations. Is it heroic to maintain a moral
stance in the face of an immoral enemy, especially
terrorists, or must one "fight fire with fire"?

3) If a hero lays claim to a higher standard of
ethical behavior, should he or she be more harshly
judged if unable to uphold that standard?

THE PROBLEM OF MODERN LEADERSHIP

It might seem a little late to ask this question after seven chapters of text, but it is a question best answered after the sources and issues you have explored.

What is the point of this book? Why should we be occupied with questions of leadership and heroism?

The answer may be implied by this admonition from the *Haggadah of Pesach:*

In every generation a person must view himself as if he came out of Egypt.	בְּכָל דּוֹר וָדוֹר חַיָּב אָדָם לִרְאוֹת אֶת עַצְמוֹ כְּאִלּוּ הוּא יָצָא מִמִּצְרָיִם.

As Jews we have a sense of the past which interacts with our sense of the present. We are both students of history and participants in it. The structure which we have preserved and which has, in turn, preserved us — *halakha* — is a legal system based on principles and precedents. We have applied those two cornerstones of the law to every aspect of our way of life in order to keep our tradition and our culture vibrant and vital, and to instruct us as we meet the future.

We have, in the past, relied primarily on the educated and faithful leaders of our people, chosen not so much by virtue of their popular appeal as by the respect of the community for their scholarship and piety. To be sure there were exceptions — some of them are discussed in this book — and just as certainly circumstances influence the effectiveness of a leader as much as anything else. However, in modern Western civilization, leaders arise not by virtue of God's word or their mastery of it, but by another glorious process called democracy.

Imagine yourself having come out of Egypt, as the *Haggadah* instructs. Would you have voted for Moses as your leader, especially after the series of trials and tribulations which the wilderness presented? Might you have supported a leader who wanted to give you more say in how things were done?

(*Bemidbar* 16:1-3)

Korach, son of Yitzhar, son of K'hat, son of Levi, took men, along with Datan and Aviram, the sons of Eliav, and On, the son of Pelet, sons of Reuven. They rose up before Moses along with two hundred fifty men, [including] princes of the people, leaders of the assembly and men of renown. They gathered against Moses and Aaron	וַיִּקַּח קֹרַח בֶּן־יִצְהָר בֶּן־קְהָת בֶּן־לֵוִי וְדָתָן וַאֲבִירָם בְּנֵי אֱלִיאָב וְאוֹן בֶּן־פֶּלֶת בְּנֵי רְאוּבֵן: וַיָּקֻמוּ לִפְנֵי מֹשֶׁה וַאֲנָשִׁים מִבְּנֵי־יִשְׂרָאֵל חֲמִשִּׁים וּמָאתָיִם נְשִׂיאֵי עֵדָה קְרִאֵי מוֹעֵד אַנְשֵׁי־שֵׁם: וַיִּקָּהֲלוּ עַל־מֹשֶׁה וְעַל־אַהֲרֹן וַיֹּאמְרוּ אֲלֵיהֶם רַב־לָכֶם כִּי כָל־הָעֵדָה כֻּלָּם קְדֹשִׁים וּבְ־ תוֹכָם יהוה וּמַדּוּעַ תִּתְנַשְּׂאוּ עַל־קְהַל יהוה.

and said to them, "You have too much [power], since all the people are holy and God is in their midst. Why did you make yourselves leaders of God's congregation?"

Moses and Aaron are vindicated by the intervention of God, who destroys Korach and his followers, placing the Israelites back in the right hands. It was a miracle, and whether or not such a miracle could recur in our own day and age, we are admonished not to rely on miracles.

In fact, there are times when democracy and *halakha* work together. In one discussion about leadership in Tractate *Brakhot*, the Sages suggest a conversation which took place between God and Moses:

(Brakhot 55a)

Rabbi Yitchak said: We do not set a leader over the community without consulting the community, as it says, "See, God has called Betzalel, [the son of Uri] by name" (*Shmot* 35:30) [to supervise the building of the tabernacle]. The Holy One said to Moses, "Is Betzalel acceptable to you?" He replied, "Master of the Universe,

אמר רבי יצחק אין מעמידין
פרנס על הצבור אלא אם
כן נמלכים בצבור שנאמר
(שמות לה) ראו קרא ה'
בשם בצלאל אמר לו
הקדוש ברוך הוא למשה
משה הגון עליך בצלאל
אמר לו רבונו של עולם אם
לפניך הגון לפני לא כל
שכן אמר לו אף על פי כן
לך אמור להם הלך ואמר

135

if he is acceptable to you, then for me he is most certainly!" [God] said, "Even so, go speak with [the Israelites]." He went and asked the Israelites, "Is Betzalel acceptable to you?" They said, "If he is acceptable to the Holy One and to you, then for us he is most certainly!"

להם לישראל הגון עליכם בצלאל אמרו לו אם לפני הקדוש ברוך הוא ולפניך הוא הגון לפנינו לא כל שכן.

There are also times when democracy and *halakha* have different goals: democracy reflects the will of the people. *Halakha* represents, as best we can understand it, the will of God. A dependence on the good will of the people is not always such a wise course of action, because a leader who must rely on the good will of the people must cultivate it.

(Ketubot 105b)

Abaye said, If a rabbinic leader is loved by the people of his community it is not because he is so great [a scholar]. Rather, it is because he doesn't criticize them on heavenly matters.

אמר אביי האי צורבא מרבנן דמרחמין ליה בני מתא לאו משום דמעלי טפי אלא משום דלא מוכח להו במילי דשמיא.

We are therefore faced with a challenge: to bring the virtues of democracy and the values of *halakha* together, to exercise our right to choose our leaders in such a way that both the process and the leader reflect, as best as possible, the ideals which our tradition holds for leadership.

Further complicating matters for us are the rules of North American governments which limit their interaction with religion. One such limitation is found in the First Amendment to the Constitution of the United States, which states, in part, "Congress shall make no law respecting an establishment of religion." Though many leaders of the United States and Canada profess deep religious convictions, the population as a whole is suspicious of religious leaders who attempt to become political leaders, whether they espouse liberal or conservative points of view. Is there a conflict between a commitment to upholding God's mandates for us and upholding the oath of secular public office?

Now is the point at which we must examine the question of who our leaders are today. Begin by making a list of the ten people you admire most. When you have completed the list, try to identify the qualities each person has which makes them your leaders, your heroes or your role models. How do they measure up to the values we have identified in our historical models?Next, make a list of the people you think are the ten most important leaders of our time. Again, try to identify the qualities which make them leaders. How do they measure up to the values we have identified in our historical models?

It has been suggested that our modern Jewish communities have produced leaders without followers and followers without leaders. No matter which organization or movement you examine, it is inevitable to hear leaders bemoan the lack of devotion of their constituency to the cause, and the constituents to criticize the leadership for lacking direction. To be sure, these complaints have been voiced by most people at most times in history. However, as mentioned earlier, we are both students of history and participants in it.

Here are some of the people — and only some — who are Jewish leaders of our time, and what they say about Jewish leadership.

Robert Gordis, Conservative rabbi and Professor of Bible: "The capstone in the arch of the rabbi's manifold activities is his role as Jewish spokesperson and community leader on the national and international scenes... The Jewish cultural equipment of the rabbi, his forensic gifts, his total absorption in Jewish affairs, his communal experience, and his prestige in the Jewish community make him an ideal public servant of the Jewish community, a statesman at his best, or, alas, merely a politician... The rabbi will stand or fall on his knowledge of Torah, his capacity to communicate the content and significance of the Jewish tradition... [W]hile I have any life and strength, I hope I can do what I can 'lehagdil Torah ulha'adirah,' to magnify the Torah and enhance it."

Leonard Fein, current contributor to and founding publisher of *Moment* magazine: "Judaism does not 'play a role' [in my life]. I am a Jew; all that I do is informed by my understanding of who I am... If I could use the full strength of my influence to effect change in Jewish society, I would transform Jewish education, in part by multiplying our investment in Jewish summer camping a hundred-fold. If I could change general society, I would forbid poverty."

Joseph Lieberman, Attorney General of the State of Connecticut: "Judaism plays an indirect but substantial role in my professional life because Jewish law, history and ethics are one of the major sources of my original interest in the law and continue to help guide my actions as a public lawyer... Among my models of Jewish leadership are Senator Rudy Boschwitz [of Minnesota] because of the way he combines his success in government with a productive commitment to the Jewish community, and Rabbi Irving Greenberg because of his commitment to Jewish unity."

Danny Siegel, poet, author, founder of *Ziv Tzedakah Fund*, former international USY president: Among the qualities a Jewish leader should have are, "first, compassion and caring for those under his leadership. After that, if the person has good administrative abilities, that's fine. But first comes the caring. And humility...My role models are mitzvah heroes; young, old, rich, medium and poor, men, women,... anyone who is applying his/her talents toward some manner of Tzedakah work...[They] run from age 11 to 87, all ranges of intelligence and occupation and education, sex, and religion..."

Letty Cottin Pogrebin, contributing editor of Ms. magazine: "A Jewish leader is someone who empowers other Jews to be more effective, humane d secure in the larger world as well as in the Jewish community... I've always felt sanctified by Judaism and Jewish history, and lucky to be born into a culture that reveres learning and turns its own suffering into humor...[but] a Jewish leader is not always male — although when the media seeks "Jewish opinion" and quotes only men it may seem that way."

Helen Suzman, Member of South Africa's Parliament and anti-apartheid leader: "I consider that I represent all my constituents, Jewish and otherwise. I do not know what qualifies an individual to be called a Jewish leader, except a leader who is Jewish... I am not a religious Jew, nor do I play any part in

Jewish community life in South Africa, though I certainly identify with the various Jewish and Zionist organizations... I do not look for role models and therefore do not have a model of Jewish leadership to whom I could refer. I am guided entirely by my own deeply held convictions and the goal of a just society... [free] of racial discrimination in all spheres."

Max M. Kampelman, United States arms treaty negotiator: "I consider one of the great contributions of Judaism to modern civilization to stem from the days of the early Hebrew tribes who proclaimed to the world their belief in a single God. This was in an atmosphere in which many different peoples and cultures thought in terms of many gods. The concept of one God meant that all of the rest of us were his children. The notion of the fatherhood of God brings with it, of course, the concept of the brotherhood of man in that all of his children are thus brothers and sisters to one another. Here is the root of what later became political democracy. I look upon political democracy as the expression of that religious concept originally developed by the ancient Hebrew tribes."

Henry A. Waxman, United States Congressman (24th District, California): "I count as a Jewish leader any Jew whose views on matters of consequence are taken seriously by a significant number of his or her co-religionists... Major sources of guidance in my work are the values of our Torah and, especially, the social teachings of the ancient Hebrew prophets. My attachment to Israel is infused with deep personal and religious sentiment far beyond pure geopolitics... I feel a spiritual as well as civic obligation to promote health care for the poor and elderly. On a more personal note, I feel strongly that the code of Jewish ethics has protected me from some of the ethical difficulties encountered by members [of Congress] concerned solely with federal law or formal congressional ethics rulings. For a politician, there are many sober lessons to be learned from the Halakhic stricture against 'mar'it ayin' — the mere *appearance* of wrongdoing."

Francine Klagsbrun, author: "Apart from religious ceremonies and rituals, apart from holidays and festivals, what endured most meaningfully for me were the texts and teachings, and the power of their ethical principles and practical insights. That core of values that is the essence of Judaism was always there for me — balanced, within reach, yet motivated by inspired ideals; and I found that these values grew rather than diminished in meaning, even as I grew and changed, even as society was transformed."

Paul Simon, singer and composer:
Silent Eyes
Watching
Jerusalem
Make her bed of stones
Silent Eyes
No one will comfort her
Jerusalem
Weeps alone
She is sorrow
Sorrow
She burns like a flame
And she calls my name
Silent Eyes
Burning
In the desert sun
Halfway to Jerusalem
And we shall all be called as witnesses
Each and every one
To stand before the eyes of God
And speak what was done

What do you think of each of the above

statements? Some of the ways you might evaluate the statements include:

• How do the quotations from these leaders in Jewish community, public service, and the arts measure up to the values identified in the historical heroes in this source book?

• How do the leaders on your list compare with these individuals?

• Would you concur that all of these ten individuals are Jewish leaders? Would you choose or reject any of them as personal role models?

Leaders of the Conservative Movement

No sourcebook on Jewish leadership would be complete without examples of leaders from within the workings of the Jewish community itself. Our own Conservative Movement has been blessed with many fine leaders who have worked to further the cause of Jewish values and practices from within the three branches of the Movement; the United Synagogue, the Rabbinical Assembly and the Jewish Theological Seminary. To illustrate the quality and accomplishments of our leaders, the three most recent elected top officials of those organizations are briefly profiled below. Each has contributed in his own way to the advancement of Conservative Judaism beyond these brief summaries, as have many other elected and non-elected leaders who have been omitted for no other reason than space limitations. Many such leaders exist within your own synagogue.

CHANCELLORS OF THE JEWISH THEOLOGICAL SEMINARY

The Jewish Theological Seminary was founded in

1886 to train new generations of rabbis and scholars for traditional Judaism in America. Over the years, it has developed into one of the foremost centers of Jewish scholarship in the world, encompassing not just the Rabbinical School, but undergraduate, graduate and post-graduate programs, as well as outreach programs to high school and college students and those studying in non-degree programs.

Dr. Louis Finkelstein served as Chancellor from 1951-1972. Already a pulpit rabbi and scholar of international renown, he used his position as professor, administrator and, later, Chancellor to train and attract top scholars with a variety of perspectives for the Seminary faculty. Dr. Finkelstein initiated innovative programs in interfaith activities, founding the Institute for Religious and Social Studies which now bears his name, and he recognized the power of the public media with the creation of the "Eternal Light" radio and television program. He was advisor to four United States Presidents. Dr. Finkelstein's research and writing in the fields of history and rabbinics continue to set the highest standards to which others aspire.

Dr. Gerson D. Cohen served as Chancellor from 1972-1986. Early in his life Dr.Cohen earned the reputation as a foremost authority in medieval Jewish history. Upon succeeding Dr. Finkelstein, he set about developing a greater depth to the graduate and undergraduate opportunities available to students, and redefining the curriculum of the Rabbinical School to meet the needs of contemporary students. Dr. Cohen oversaw the development of the Seminary's campus in Los Angeles, the University of Judaism, and the completion of the Seminary quadrangle in New York, including a new library to replace the one destroyed years earlier in a tragic fire. Dr. Cohen led a team of scholars who studied the issue of ordaining women as rabbis, and presided over the Seminary faculty which voted to admit women to the Rabbinical School based on that study's conclusions.

Dr. Ismar Schorsch is the current Chancellor. Having established his credentials as a respected historian, and after serving as Provost in Dr. Cohen's administration, Dr. Schorsch has presided over the Seminary's Centennial and is preparing for the ordination of the first Israeli Conservative rabbis in our history. In his brief tenure, Dr. Schorsch has taken firm hold of the Chancellorship, as evidenced by his controversial decision to ordain women as cantors, using as his reasoning the scholarship and experience of those who endorsed the ordination of women as rabbis.

PRESIDENTS OF THE RABBINICAL ASSEMBLY

The Rabbinical Assembly is the official organization of Conservative Rabbis in Israel, the United States, Canada, Europe, and South America. Its membership numbers over 1000, most of whom were ordained by the Jewish Theological Seminary. In addition to serving as a forum for professional concerns, the Rabbinical Assembly addresses matters of Jewish law, social justice and public policy through its committees, and coordinates continuing educational opportunities for its members through publications and conferences.

Rabbi Arnold Goodman served as President from 1982-1984. Currently the rabbi of Congregation Ahavath Achim in Atlanta, Rabbi Goodman also holds a law degree. One of the areas in which Rabbi Goodman has taken a leadership role has been in the practice of mourning and burial procedures, as chronicled in the film and book "A Plain Pine Box," the story of his work with the *Chevra Kaddisha* of Adath Jeshurun in Minneapolis, where he previously served.

Rabbi Alexander Shapiro served as President from 1984-1986. Rabbi Shapiro is currently the rabbi of Oheb Shalom Congregation in South Orange, New Jersey. Rabbi Shapiro has taken the lead in matters of social justice, dating back to his involvement with the civil rights movement of the early 1960's and continuing in the efforts of his administration to rebuild bridges with the black community and to address matters of social inequality in North and South American and Israeli societies.

Rabbi Kassel Abelson currently serves as President. His long career at Beth El Congregation in Minneapolis has earned him the reputation as "a rabbi's rabbi." Rabbi Abelson has demonstrated the range of his leadership skills in his administration's support for direct action on matters of social conscience involving Soviet Jewry, oppressed Jewish communities, American politics and, most especially, the development of Conservative Judaism in Israel. He has also been instrumental in developing and supporting USY during his entire career. During Rabbi Abelson's administration, the Rabbinical Assembly and United Synagogue introduced *Siddur Sim Shalom*, edited by Rabbi Jules Harlow.

PRESIDENTS OF UNITED SYNAGOGUE OF AMERICA

United Synagogue of America is the lay (non-professional) arm of the Conservative Movement, representing over 800 congregations which identify with our philosophy and practice of Judaism. Through the involvement of its constituent congregations and their volunteer leadership, the organization and its professional staff provide programmatic, educational and adminstrative service to its membership and represent the concerns of our movement and tradition to the community at large. The Department of Youth Activities, publisher of this source book, directs the activities of Kadima and USY, among other things.

Simon Schwartz of Tom's River, New Jersey, served as President from 1977-1981. Mr. Schwartz's management skills saw United Synagogue through trying times. His efforts to strengthen the organization, both financially and in terms of lay involvement, gave United Synagogue renewed vigor in its task of serving its membership. Of particular concern to Mr. Schwartz has been our Zionist philosophy, which he translated into action, as demonstrated by his current position as President of MERCAZ (Movement to Reaffirm Conservative Zionism), the third-largest delegation to the World Zionist Congress.

Marshall Wolke of Chicago was President from 1981-1985. Mr. Wolke's priority was the expansion of services, especially in the areas of youth and education. With his support, hundreds of thousands of dollars were channeled into youth programming and educational resources. During this time, the Solomon Schechter Day School network expanded to seventy schools in North America. Mr. Wolke also helped focus the attention of the organization on the needs of special populations, including singles and young leadership, and on matters of public policy. Today he serves as President of the World Council of Synagogues, which assists in the organization and funding of developing Conservative congregations outside of North America.

Franklin D. Kreutzer of Miami is currently President. Mr. Kreutzer typifies the "activist" style of leadership, bringing the organization and its values closer to individual members by traveling tirelessly to every United Synagogue Region and meeting with local and regional leaders to strengthen the unity of United Synagogue. Mr. Kreuzter's personal commitments to observance led him to form the Committee on Commitment and Observance, designed to increase the level of Jewish practice among the lay people. His concern for the future of our people is evident through his administration's commission on drug and alcohol abuse by Jews and by increased emphasis on addressing issues of marriage in the American Jewish community. Mr. Kreutzer has been aggressive in articulating his vision of United Synagogue and the Conservative Movement.

OBVERSE

In the centre, the verse from the Song of David, "He sent from above and took me," "Psalms 18, Verse 17" in Hebrew and English.

REVERSE

In the centre, the emblem of Zahal (Israel Defense Forces) the sword with olive leaf and branch entwined superimposed on the wings of an airplane, with the Star of David on the left wing. On the bottom, the inscription in Hebrew and English, "Operation Jonathan, 4th 1976."

Chapter 9

WHO ARE OUR JEWISH HEROES TODAY?

In 1963, the Los Angeles Dodgers and the New York Yankees met in baseball's World Series. On the pitching staff for the Dodgers was a young Jew named Sandy Koufax. Koufax was one of the best pitchers in all of baseball history, and 1963 was when he was at his peak. The coincidence of the schedule had one game — a game Koufax was to pitch — occur on *Yom Kippur*.

Sandy Koufax refused to pitch that game.

A great deal of attention was shifted to Sandy Koufax and his religious convictions, almost all of it positive. In fact, one of the Yankees good-naturedly suggested that the following game was also on a Jewish holiday: "Yom Koufax". A surge of pride in being Jewish swept through America, thanks to this public demonstration of respect for the sanctity of the holiest day of the year.

Was Sandy Koufax a Jewish hero?

On the face of it, you might be inclined to say he was. Bearing in mind our original definition of a hero — a person whose special and specific action, whose extra effort at a crucial moment set an example toward which we aspire — Sandy Koufax seems to meet our criteria. In the context of 1963 America, Sandy Koufax was indeed a Jewish hero.

However, Sandy Koufax spent that *Yom Kippur* in his uniform, sitting on the bench in the Dodger dug-out to support his teammates. He pitched every *Shabbat*, every *Shavu'ot*, every *Tisha B'Av* he was assigned. In other circumstances, the level of Koufax's observance might have brought him nothing but criticism from his fellow Jews.

As the historical examples have amply demonstrated, circumstance and opportunity play as much a role in heroism as the character of the hero. Rachav's betrayal of her city, Bar Kokhba's insurrection, Rabbi Meir of Rotenburg's refusal of funds might have been judged very differently were Rachav a Jew in Jerusalem, Bar Kokhba a member of a Jewish self-defense group in America, or Rabbi Meir the director of an inner-city *yeshivah*!

We must therefore seek to evaluate heroes in their own contexts — and leaders as well — while remaining conscious of the Jewish values they represent.

When I was eleven years old, I would have done just about anything for a chance to pitch in the World Series. Sandy Koufax's heroism taught me a lesson I never forgot.

Heroes are often where you look for them. Here, then, are just a few of the heroes of our generation, and a brief description of what made them heroes. Try to identify the Jewish values exemplified by each. How did their actions benefit the Jews? Did their heroics also benefit the greater society? Would you have advised each person to have done what he or she did had you been asked? Would you identify each person as a Jewish hero?

Hadassah Levi is the founder and director of

Ma'on Latinok in Israel. *Ma'on Latinok* and Hadassah's involvement with the organization is described in Danny Siegel's *Ziv Tzedakah Fund* report of April 1, 1987: "Last summer Hadassah explained to me the origins of the Ma'on....When she was hospitalized for a lengthy stretch years back, she noticed infants with Down's Syndrome that had been left behind in the hospital. She was convinced she could offer them a full, meaningful life under her care. She swore that, if she recovered from her own illness, she would raise these children herself. Her nearly forty children now range from ages 7 to 10. Hadassah's lease on the old Ma'on was up, and she has temporarily housed them in a government institution in Jerusalem, while she continues a search for a new home....We hope that by the summer it will happen."

Judith Resnick was an astronaut on the space shuttle Challenger. She was killed in the tragic explosion which claimed the lives of the entire crew. Though she was a member of a synagogue youth group as a child, in her adult life she did not identify ith the Jewish community.

Jonathan Netanyahu was commander of a hostage rescue unit of the Israel Defense Forces. In June of 1976, a group of terrorists hijacked an Air France jet and flew it to Uganda. There they released the non-Jewish passengers and held the Jews (who were citizens of many countries) hostage. Netanyahu's unit flew secretly to Entebbe, Uganda and rescued all of the hostages on July 4. Only one Jewish life was lost — Jonathan Netanyahu. (A collection of his letters was published as *Self-Portrait of a Hero*, Random House, 1980).

Abraham Joshua Heschel was a brilliant and forceful rabbi and philosopher who found within

Judaism the mandate to speak out with great urgency on issues of social justice. It was Heschel who first brought the plight of Soviet Jewry to the attention of the American community in 1962, who worked closely with Pope John XXIII to reformulate the Catholic teachings on Jews and Judaism, who helped inspire President Kennedy to convene conferences on Aging and on Children. Perhaps the most heroic act of his career was commited when he walked arm-in-arm with Dr. Martin Luther King, Jr. in a civil rights demonstration in Selma, Alabama — a striking figure with a mane of white hair, becoming a symbol of Jewish activism for generations. Professor Heschel combined a lifelong devotion to scholarship with a passion for social justice which often led him to take controversial moral stands.

Avital and Natan Sharansky were married in the USSR in 1974. The next day, Avital left for Israel and Natan (then Anatoly) continued to wait for permission to join her. In 1977, he was arrested and sentenced to thirteen years in prison. While he endured torture, isolation and deprivation, she campaigned tirelessly for his release and the cause of Soviet Jewry. In 1986, they were reunited and now live in Jerusalem. On the day of his sentencing, he said, "Five years ago I submitted my application for exit to Israel. Now I am further than ever from my dream. It would seem to be cause for regret. But it is absolutely otherwise. I am happy. I am happy that I lived honestly, in peace with my conscience. I never compromised my soul, even under the threat of death..."

Phil Pill was an officer of International USY and a rock musician. He and his band traveled to Vietnam in 1968 to entertain American troops fighting a very controversial war. He was killed when the jeep in which he and his band were traveling was ambushed by enemy guerillas.

Joanne Greenberg has written a number of novels (including *I Never Promised You a Rose Garden*) and collections of short stories, (including *High Crimes and Misdemeanors*), which are devoted to Jewish themes. Though she makes her living as a writer, she also was the first woman officer of the Lookout Mountain Fire Department Highland Rescue Squad in her hometown of Golden, Colorado. During her thirteen years on the team as an emergency medical technician she arranged with another member of the squad who was a devoted Christian to cover his Sunday obligations in exchange for her *Shabbat* duty. She made over 1,000 "runs" as a paramedic, assisting in everything from traffic accidents to a cattle roundup on an interstate highway to barely outrunning a raging forest fire. Perhaps the most dramatic rescue in which she participated was that of a three year old child who was discovered by accident in an outdoor privy. She had been kidnapped, abused and left for dead. Greenberg and her partner saved the little girl's life.

Elie Wiesel is a Nobel Prize-winning historian, scholar and writer who has eloquently and compellingly born witness to the Holocaust. He was presented with the Congressional Medal of Freedom by President Ronald Reagan days before the President was to visit a cemetery in Bitburg, Germany in which were buried members of Hitler's SS. Wiesel, speaking to the President in the White House, on national television, urged him not to go, saying, "Your place, Mr. President, is not there. Your place is with the victims."

Lee Kweller was handicapped as an infant in 1972 with cerebral palsy. He can neither walk nor talk. After he and his mother worked with Dr. John

Eulenberg, a Jewish research scientist at Michigan State University's Artificial Language Laboratory, Lee celebrated his bar mitzvah in November 1985 by using a speech synthesizer controlled by computer. His *parasha* was *Vayyera*, and the *haftarah* was II Kings 4:1-37, the story of how Elisha the prophet revived the dead son of a pious woman. Speaking both English and Hebrew for the first time in his life, Lee said, "The *haftarah* this week tells of a child coming back to life because of the dedication of a great woman. I, too, have come to life today, both in the tradition of my forefathers and in a very special way. I am now able to speak with all of you. This marks the beginning of a new world for me. Because the people around me expect the best from me, I have grown and gained confidence in myself. I believe that I can accomplish anything in this world."

Try to identify ten Jewish heroes of your own.

LEADERSHIP IN YOUR OWN WORLD

In the book of *B'reishit* are two verses which use similar language to describe two different people:

(B'reishit 6:9b-c)

Noah was a man who was righteous and whole-hearted in his generation. Noah walked with God.

נֹחַ אִישׁ צַדִּיק תָּמִים הָיָה בְּדֹרֹתָיו אֶת־הָאֱלֹהִים הִתְהַלֶּךְ־נֹחַ׃

(B'reishit 17:1b-c)

...God said [to Avram]: I am Eil-Shaddai. Walk before me and be whole-hearted.

וַיֵּרָא יהוה אֶל־אַבְרָם וַיֹּאמֶר אֵלָיו אֲנִי־אֵל שַׁדַּי הִתְהַלֵּךְ לְפָנַי וֶהְיֵה תָמִים׃

Both Noah and Avram (Abraham) are described in the Torah as whole-hearted, that is, both free from dishonesty and filled with integrity. The idea of each of them walking in God's presence, an image of their

155

loyalty to God and spiritual depth, is also used in each
description.

There are differences in the descriptions,
however: Noah was whole-hearted *in his generation.*
And while Noah walked *with God,* Avram walked
before God.

Those differences were not overlooked by the
scholars of any period of history. Rashi, perhaps the
most famous commentator on the *Tenakh,* summed
up the discussions which take place in the
commentaries in his typically brief and effective way:

(Rashi on B'reishit 6:9)

"In his generation:" Some of our sages interpret this word to his benefit: He would have been that much more righteous in a generation of righteous people! Some interpret it to his detriment: Compared to his generation, he was righteous, but had he been in Abraham's generation, he would have been considered a nothing!

בְּדֹרֹתָיו. יֵשׁ מֵרַבּוֹתֵינוּ
דּוֹרְשִׁים אוֹתוֹ לְשֶׁבַח, כָּל
שֶׁכֵּן אִלּוּ הָיָה בְּדוֹר
צַדִּיקִים הָיָה צַדִּיק יוֹתֵר:
וְיֵשׁ שֶׁדּוֹרְשִׁים אוֹתוֹ
לִגְנַאי, לְפִי דוֹרוֹ הָיָה
צַדִּיק, וְאִלּוּ הָיָה בְּדוֹרוֹ
שֶׁל אַבְרָהָם לֹא הָיָה
נֶחְשָׁב לִכְלוּם.

Were we to phrase the dispute in the terms of
this source book, the question might be, Is a leader
produced by his or her environment, or is a leader one
who rises above that environment? We might very
well ask that question about each of the leaders in this
book.

Were it just for the phrase "in his generation,"

we might not find an answer to the question. Rashi, however, summed up the discussions on the other comparison of descriptions.

(Ibid.)

"Noah walked with God." But about Abraham it said [he] walked before God. Noah needed help to support himself, but Abraham found internal strength and walked in his righteousness by himself.

אֶת הָאֱלֹהִים הִתְהַלֶּךְ נֹחַ. וּבְאַבְרָהָם הוּא אוֹמֵר: אֲשֶׁר הִתְהַלַּכְתִּי לְפָנָיו. (בראשית כ"ד), נֹחַ הָיָה צָרִיךְ סַעַד לְתָמְכוֹ; אֲבָל אַבְרָהָם הָיָה מִתְחַזֵּק וּמְהַלֵּךְ בְּצִדְקוֹ מֵאֵלָיו:

The statement is clear: Noah was a leader for his generation, but not up to the standard of a different generation.

Before coming down too hard on Noah, it is worthwhile to remember an important fact in biblical history: were it not for Noah with his lower level of righteousness and whole-heartedness, the generation of the Flood would have been without survivors, and there would have been no Abraham — and, for that matter, nobody else. By behaving in a consistently positive way and remaining as faithful as he could in his own way to the principles in which he believed, Noah literally saved the entire world from extinction. He did so without being *the best that ever was.* He did so by being the best *he could be.*

Each of the leaders in this book was, first and foremost, a human being, and was, therefore, imperfect. From Deborah to the contemporary leaders in chapter 8, every generation's leaders have had their acknowledged flaws. Even the greatest (and in some ways most mysterious) leader of our people, the unique Moses, was decidedly human and unable to deal with some of the challenges he faced.

It should also be obvious to you that a great part of the success of a leader rests with the people he or she is attempting to lead. If effectiveness of the leader is measured by the quality of his or her guidance, then it is not really important to dwell on the quantity of a leader's followers.

Take, for example, your own circle of friends. No matter how close you might be with each other, it is likely that one or two stand out as the most influential in your group. They are the ones whose opinion counts most when you are deciding between pizza and ice cream, between bowling and a movie, between dungarees and dressy clothes. In fact, your own group of friends and its leaders may have more of an influence on the way you act and think than any of the leaders or heroes you listed in chapters 8 and 9.

Those same peer leaders influence their friends in matters of personal behavior: sexual activity, substance abuse, respect for property and respect for other people. They help to shape day-to-day behavior toward authority figures: parents, teachers, police, youth leaders. You may be one of those leaders; you may be among the followers. Most likely, you are sometimes a leader and sometimes a follower.

Can you think of examples in which you or someone else tried to lead your friends to do something they did not want to do right away? Was the activity something "good" or something "bad"? In what ways did the leader try to influence the others? Was the leader successful? What was the result of the effort?

Similarly, a family unit has leaders and followers. In general, it is the parents who lead and the children who follow. The first paragraph of the *Shema* clearly instructs parents to lead their families when it says to take God's words to heart, "teach them to your children, speaking of them at home and away, when you lie down and when you arise." Just as clearly, children are to show deference to their parents, as the fifth commandment states.

There may be times when that relationship changes. Parents will sometimes look for guidance from their children in understanding modern technology, popular music or fashion. It will sometimes happen that a young person will rediscover the beauty and depth of Jewish tradition and develop a level of commitment to observance which is different from his or her parents. Very often the commitment comes as a result of experiences in a youth group like USY or a summer experience like USY Israel Pilgrimage, USY-on-Wheels or Camp Ramah. Upon returning home, the child may seek to lead the family toward a similar level of commitment.

As parents age, children often change roles with them, giving their parents more and more care and receiving less in return. The plaintive prayer we recite during the High Holy Days, "do not cast us off in our old age when our strength has diminished," has special meaning for anyone who has ever seen beloved parents or grandparents become increasingly dependent as they grow old.

Can you think of examples in your own family in which two members have tried to lead it in different directions? What were the results? Were the discussions (or, perhaps, arguments) focused on the different directions, or were there issues of leadership at the core?

It is unusual for any individual to lead a nation, an army or even a large group of people. Most leaders — and most of us are leaders at some point — find themselves leading peer groups and families. Peer groups may be school friends, organized clubs, co-workers on the job, residents in a college dormitory or members of an athletic team. Families may consist of father, mother, children and relatives from other nuclear families, or they may be some smaller combination of any of those people.

Each of us, at some point, is called upon to be like Noah.

Return to the chapters on leaders. How might you apply the Jewish values expressed in their examples to your opportunities to lead?

Chapter 11

HEROISM IN YOUR OWN WORLD

The title of this source book was taken from the very first source quoted in it:

(Pirkei Avot 4:1)

Ben Zoma said... Who is a hero? One who conquers his passion...

בֶּן זוֹמָא אוֹמֵר: אֵיזֶהוּ גִבּוֹר הַכּוֹבֵשׁ אֶת־יִצְרוֹ.

Yet, it seems that most of the heroes presented as examples were not people who controlled their impulses, but those who gave them expression in some exceptional form. Is Ben Zoma's advice merely a quaint little saying, or is it truly an insight into the nature of heroism?

One answer is found in *Avot d'Rabbi Natan,* a very old commentary on *Pirkei Avot,* the source of Ben Zoma's quotation. The author comments:

(Avot d'Rabbi Natan Ch.23)

Who is the hero of heroes?..
Some say one who makes
an enemy into his friend.

איזה גבור שבגבורים...
יש אומרים מי שעושה
שונא אוהבו:

The word for "enemy" used in this quotation
means "one who hates". It is unclear whether the
"one who hates" is the person him- or herself, or
whether it is another person. It is just as unclear
whether the hero of heroes makes the other person
into a friend or acts as a friend to the other person.
What do the differences in understanding the
commentary mean to your understanding of Ben
Zoma?
Another comment is found in the writings of
Rabbi Jonah ben Abraham Gerondi, who lived in the
first half of the thirteenth century. He was known for
his writings on ethical behavior and personal morality.

(Rabbenu Yonah on Pirke Avot 4:1)

Just as physical strength
elevates [the body] and im-
proves it, so, too, spiritual
strength elevates [the soul].
Both people and animals have
physical strength, for both can
lift heavy loads, some more
than others. But Ben Zoma is
not talking about such
[strength]. Rather, heroism
refers to inner strength..., the
strength to conquer one's

כמו שכח הגוף היא
מעלתו וחשיבותו. כך
כח הנשמה הוא
מעלתה. וגבורת הגוף
שהיא הכח באדם גם
בבהמה הוא כי לכלם
יש כח לישא משאות
ומהם יותר על
חבריהם. ובזה לא דבר
בן זומא כי לא נקראת

162

passions, and this is what separates human beings from animals, for animals have no such inner strength.

גבורה אך מגבורת הלב... וגם כח כבישת היצר והיא נחלקת בין האדם והבהמה כי לא לבהמות גבורת הלב.

It seems that Ben Zoma, Rabbi Natan and Rabbenu Yonah all consider the greatest type of heroism to be that which is considered, reasoned and controlled — not at all impulsive.

The fact of the matter is, in light of all we have studied, they are correct. Each of the heroes, from Judah to Judah Loew, from Bar Kokhba to Elie Wiesel acted not on impulse but out of his or her considered understanding of the situation. The football player who catches the touchdown pass has spent a whole season training for that moment; the soldier who stops the advancing enemy has been prepared to handle himself in combat; the person who rebukes the bigot has cultivated values and principles which readied her for that opportunity. When circumstances present themselves, heroes respond more often than not out of a certain wisdom gained through experience, wisdom which has become so much a part of themselves that their response is almost a reflex.

It is that inner strength of spirit — *gevurat halev*, as Rabbenu Yonah terms it — which creates the potential for heroism. It is the unique circumstance of a person's life — your life — which creates opportunities for heroism.

How can a person prepare to become a hero?

(*Mishlei* 19:16)

One who keeps a *mitzvah* keeps his life.

שֹׁמֵר מִצְוָה שֹׁמֵר נַפְשׁוֹ.

(Pirkei Avot 4:11)

Rabbi Eliezer ben Ya'akov said, A person who does a single *mitzvah* acquires an advocate for himself.

רַבִּי אֱלִיעֶזֶר בֶּן יַעֲקֹב אוֹמֵר: הָעוֹשֶׂה מִצְוָה אַחַת קוֹנֶה לוֹ פְּרַקְלִיט אֶחָד.

(Yoma 39a)

A person who raises his level of holiness just a little will be raised by it a lot.

אדם מקדש עצמו מעט מקדשין אותו הרבה.

There is similar advice to be found in all quarters of Jewish wisdom, and it boils down to this:

Start by becoming an expert in a single *mitzvah*. Whether you make it your specialty to alert your representative in government about the plight of Syrian Jews or to read Torah, to tie *tzitzit* or to listen to a despairing friend, you will sow the seeds of heroism in your own life.

It was not easy to impress the sages of the Talmud. Yet, a man named Elazar ben Durdia became something of a hero to them by virtue of a single *mitzvah*, one solitary act of personal heroism. Elazar ben Durdia was a highly promiscuous person, willing to travel great distances for a one-night stand. Apparently, his reputation caught up with him, because one night a woman said to him that he would never be forgiven his immorality. The effect on him was immediate.

He went and sat between two [ranges of] mountains and hills. He said to them, "Mountains and hills, seek mercy for me." They said to him, "How can we ask for you; we should ask for ourselves, as it says: For the mountains may be displaced and the hills shaken... (Isaiah 54:10)." He said, "Heavens and earth, seek mercy for me." They said to him, "How can we ask for you; we should ask for ourselves, as it says: For the heavens shall disperse like smoke and the earth shall wear out like clothing... (Isaish 51:6)." He said, "Sun and moon, seek mercy for me." They said to him, "How can we ask for you; we should ask for ourselves as it says: The moon shall be ashamed and the sun embarassed... (Isaiah 24:23)." He said, "Stars and constellations, seek mercy for me." They said to him, "How can we ask for you; we should ask for ourselves, as it says: The whole regiment of the sky shall shrivel... (Isaiah 34:4)." He said, "The matter rests with me alone." He hung his

הלך וישב בין שני הרים
וגבעות אמר הרים
וגבעות בקשו עלי רחמים
אמרו לו עד שאנו
מבקשים עליך נבקש על
עצמנו שנאמר (ישעיה
נד) כי ההרים ימושו
והגבעות תמוטינה אמר
שמים וארץ בקשו עלי
רחמים אמרו עד שאנו
מבקשים עליך נבקש על
עצמנו שנאמר (שם נא)
כי שמים כעשן נמלחו
והארץ כבגד תבלה אמר
חמה ולבנה בקשו עלי
רחמים אמרו לו עד
שאנו מבקשים עליך
נבקש על עצמנו שנאמר
(שם כד) וחפרה הלבנה
ובושה החמה אמר
כוכבים ומזלות בקשו עלי
רחמים אמרו לו עד
שאנו מבקשים עליך
נבקש על עצמנו שנאמר
(שם לד) ונמקו כל צבא
השמים אמר אין הדבר
תלוי אלא בי הניח ראשו
בין ברכיו וגעה בבכיה
עד שיצתה נשמתו יצתה
בת קול ואמרה ר"א בן

head between his knees and cried in agony until his soul departed. A voice from heaven came out and said, "Rabbi Elazar ben Durdia has been invited to everlasting life..." Rabbi [Yehudah Ha Nasi:] said, "Not only does God receive the penitent, but they are called 'Rabbi.'"

דורדיא מזומן לחיי העולם הבא... ואמר רבי לא דיין לבעלי תשובה שמקבלין אותן אלא שקורין אותן רבי.

Elazar ben Durdia reached down inside to find his *gevurat lev*, and thereby redeemed himself from self-pity. He discovered a profound truth — "the matter rests with me alone" — and once he sincerely performed the *mitzvah* of repentance, he found himself elevated to the status of rabbi, of role model to others. The point of the story is not Elazar's death — it is Elazar's immediate acceptance by God.

There are times when living life itself is heroic. Whether the circumstances are of your own making or whether they are beyond your control, it sometimes takes *gevurat lev* to greet each day.

Jews in many countries know the terror of political oppression. In the Soviet Union and other Eastern Bloc countries, in many Arab countries, even in South and Central America, it can be dangerous to identify as a Jew. Certainly others face similar challenges due to racial or religious prejudices. In what ways can a person in such a situation be a hero?

People who have physical or mental disabilities which impair their access to many activities we think of as "normal" also draw on an internal spiritual strength. Fortunately, we have all become more aware of physical barriers which impede the disabled. Too often the prejudices of able people close doors of social contact to the disabled, or label them unfairly as unable to participate in the simple joys of day-to-day life. What are the kinds of heroism required of someone disabled?

Chemical dependencies also call for a special kind of heroism on the part of the dependent person. Like other compulsive behaviors — gambling, doing violence to self or others, lying — alcohol and other drugs create a personal prison from which it becomes harder and harder for a person to be released. Our tradition calls *pidyon sh'vuyim* (ransoming hostages) one of the most important *mitzvot*. How might this *mitzvah* become a vehicle of heroism for the chemically dependent person?

These few extreme examples may lead you to believe that the circumstances of your own life, if free from such influences, may not afford you the chance to act heroically. Of course, we know that no one's life is without troubles and obstacles. With greater or lesser frequency, everyone feels at times that the world is overwhelming, and the likelihood of just making it through a difficult period is small. In moments of clear thinking, each of us knows that one day is followed by the next, bringing a fresh start for new opportunities. There are times, however, when the pressures of the moment brought on by our expectations of ourselves, or the expectations of others, can cloud the hope of tomorrow.

At such a time it is well to remember one *mitzvah* which, on its surface, seems simple to understand, but may be difficult to uphold:

(Vayikra 19:18b)

... You shall love your neighbor as yourself. וְאָהַבְתָּ לְרֵעֲךָ כָּמוֹךְ

It is not the love of your neighbor which requires a certain *gevurat lev*, but the last clause of the verse, "as yourself". The Torah makes self-esteem a necessary condition for harmonious relations with others, an ideal to which we all aspire. Before a person can love his or her neighbor, that person must be able to love him- or herself.

Such self-respect is mandated in the Talmud as well, when we are instructed:

(Yevamot 25b)

A person may not make himself out to be wicked. אין אדם משים עצמו רשע

What are those things that this teaching restricts?

How does one go about developing a positive self-image?

How does the performance of this *mitzvah* make a person a hero?

A CONCLUDING WORD

This source book ends where it began, with the teaching of Ben Zoma. Just as the conclusion of the cycle of Torah readings is the beginning of a new cycle of learning, the return to Ben Zoma's definition is the beginning of a new challenge to you, the reader.

The challenge also comes from the teachings in *Pirkei Avot*, from Rabbi Joshua ben Perachya, who said:

(Pirkei Avot 1:6)

Make yourself a teacher and get yourself a friend...

עֲשֵׂה לְךָ רַב, וּקְנֵה לְךָ חָבֵר.

I leave it to you to decide whether Rabbi Joshua meant you should make yourself into a teacher or you should make someone else your teacher, whether by making yourself a teacher you get a friend or the two are different people, whether his advice is to limit yourself to a single teacher and a single friend or to apply the teaching to everyone you meet.

No matter how you interpret Rabbi Joshua's teaching, one conclusion should become apparent: at any given moment, you are someone's teacher and you are someone's friend. That also means that at those very same moments you are someone's leader, showing her the way and helping her express her goals; you are someone's hero, responding to him in a particular situation and providing for him that extra effort.

Many times that person is someone you know. Sometimes it is someone you have never met. Often, it is yourself.

Ben Zoma taught: Who is a hero? One who conquers his passion.

HEBREW GLOSSARY

aggadah — lit. "telling" or "story"; a midrash which illustrates a lesson about values or ethics

agunah — lit. "one who is anchored"; a married woman whose husband has either disappeared or has refused to divorce her

alef-bet — Hebrew alphabet (from the names of the first two letters)

aron kodesh — lit. "holy ark"; originally the resting place of the tablets of the Ten Commandments, now used to refer to the place in the synagogue in which the Torah scrolls are stored

av bet din — lit. "father of the court"; title given to the second officer of the Sanhedrin

bemidbar — lit. "in the wilderness"; the fourth book of the Torah; Numbers

ben — lit. "son"; when preceding a name it means "son of"

binyan ha'aretz — lit. "building the land"; the mitzvah of contributing materially to the reclamation, support and welfare of the Land of Israel

brakhah — lit. "blessing"; the formula recited before specific acts to make those acts sacred; plural: brakhot

b'reishit — lit. "in the beginning"; the first book of the Torah; Genesis

brit milah — lit. "covenant of circumcision"; ritual performed on male Jewish babies on the eighth day after birth (and on male Jews by choice upon conversion) signifying the pact of loyalty made between God and Abraham for all generations

devarim — lit. "words"; the fifth book of the Torah; Deuteronomy

etrog — a citrus fruit, similar to a lemon, used in the rituals of the festival of Sukkot

eretz yisrael — the Land of Israel

haggadah — lit. "telling"; the book which describes the ritual for the first nights of Pesach

halakhah — Jewish law; also used in contrast to "aggadah" to indicate a midrash used to illustrate a point of law

hallel — Psalms 113 through 118 (plus some other readings) recited on holidays in special praise of God

harav — see "rav"

kabbalah — lit. "received"; the tradition of Jewish mysticism

kokhav — lit. "star"

lulav — lit. "palm"; the branches of palm willow and myrtle trees used in the rituals of the festival of Sukkot

mashiach — lit. "anointed one"; the leader ordained by anointing with oil to be ruler, military commander and/or religious leader, also understood by some to mean the God-ordained individual who will redeem the Jews and the world from all their troubles

midrash — lit. "interpretation"; an interpretation, usually of a biblical passage, though sometimes of an event or point of law, which illustrates a lesson and may be the basis for establishing halakhah; plural: midrashim

mishnah — lit. "teaching" or "repetition"; a statement of law based on application of Torah to real situations; developed between approximately 100 BCE and 200 CE, the collection of (plural) mishnayot is divided thematically into six major sections called "sedarim" or "orders" and then "masekhtot" or "tractates;" one of the two bodies of legal literature (with gemara) which make up the Talmud

mishneh torah — lit. "repetition of the Torah"; composed by Moses Maimonides in 1180, the first code of halakhah which distilled the Talmud into easy reference form

mitzvah — lit. "commandment"; an act required of the Jew by virtue of God's command as understood by our sages; plural: mitzvot

mar'it ayin — lit. "as the eye sees"; the Jewish value which cautions the individual to consider how one's actions might appear to others

moreinu — lit. "our teacher"; an honorific title given to prestigious scholars

nasi — lit. "prince"; also the title given to the head of the Sanhedrin

omer — name of a measurement of grain brought as a daily offering in the Temple each day for seven weeks starting with the second day of Pesach

pesach — lit. "pass over"; the spring festival of freedom: Passover

pidyon shevuyim — lit. "redeeming captives"; the mitzvah of rescuing Jews who have been captured and held hostage

piku'ach nefesh — lit. "clearing rubble to find a

person" or "saving a life"; the mitzvah of preserving endangered life or safety

pirkei avot — lit. "the chapters of the fathers"; popular name for tractate Avot in the Talmud containing wisdom and aphorisms of many of the sages

Rashi — acronym for Rabbi Sh'lomo ben Yitzchak, eleventh-century French commentator on Tenakh and Talmud

rabbi — lit. "my teacher"; title given to scholars, especially in mishnaic times

rav — lit. "teacher"; title given to scholars, especially in Talmudic times; with the prefix "ha-" means "the teacher"

rosh hashanah — lit. "head of the year"; Jewish New Year

sanhedrin — the assembly of sages authorized to legislate for the entire Jewish people in Rabbinic times

shabbat — lit. "Sabbath" or "resting"; seventh day of the week on which Jews refrain from specific creative labors in order to commemorate the completion of God's original work of creation through worship, study, festive meals and rest

shacharit — lit. "dawn"; morning worship

shavuot — lit. "weeks"; the festival of first fruits and of giving of the Torah occurring seven weeks after the beginning of Pesach at the end of counting the omer

sh'lom bayit — lit. "peace of the house"; the Jewish value of harmonious relations among members of a household, group or community

sh'ma — lit. "hear" or "understand"; first word of the credo of Jewish belief: Hear O Israel, the Lord is our

God, the Lord   Alone (and subsequent biblical passages)

sh'mot — lit. "names"; the second book of Torah; Exodus

shofar — lit. "horn"; the ram's horn once sounded in battle and times of warning as well as during the season of penitence preceding Yom Kippur, as it is today

talmud — lit. "learning"; the compilation of teachings of law (mishnah) and explanatory and expansionary commentary (gemara) divided into six major topical orders each consisting of numerous sub-topical tractates; two versions exist: the Babylonian and Palestinian (or Jerusalem), each compiled in the respective centers of Jewish scholarship

NOTE: All references to Talmudic tractates in this volume are from the Babylonian Talmud unless otherwise noted

talmud torah — lit. "learning the law"; the mitzvah of studying and supporting Torah

tehillim — lit. "psalms"

tefillin — ritually constructed leather boxes containing passages from Torah commanding their use which are affixed to the arm and head during weekday morning worship

tenakh — acronym for Torah, Nevi'im, Ketuvim (Torah, Prophets, Writings), the three major divisions of the Bible; the Bible

tikkun olam — lit. "perfecting the world"; Jewish value of improving the quality of life and its many contexts

tisha b'av — lit. "ninth of (the month) Av"; day on which each of the Temples was destroyed and on which other major catastrophes have occured, creating a national day of mourning for the Jews

torah — lit. "law"; the Five Books of Moses; also, the tradition as recorded in both Tenakh and the Talmud; also, all of Jewish learning

tzahal — acronym for "tz'va haganah l'yisrael"; lit. "Israel Defense Forces"

tzedakah — lit. "righteousness"; the mitzvah which requires Jews to help those less fortunate with material and physical assistance

tzitzit — lit. "fringes"; the ritually prescribed fringes found in each of the four corners of a tallit (prayer shawl)

vayikra — lit. "he called"; the third book of Torah; Leviticus

yichus — lit. "relating"; word used to indicate lineage and/or ancestry

yom kippur — lit. "day of atonement"; holiest day of the year